Marketing of Agriculture and Allied Commodities in North East India

Marketing of Agriculture and Allied Commodities in North East India

With Special Reference to Mizoram

James L.T. Thanga

ANSHAH Anshah Publishing House

Rs. 495; US$ 24.75

ISBN: 978-81-8364-107-4

First Published in India in 2016

Marketing of Agriculture and Allied Commodities in North East India: With Special Reference to Mizoram

Published by:
ANSHAH PUBLISHING HOUSE
LG, Pankaj Central Market, I.P. Ext.,
Patparganj, Delhi-110092, Tel: 22235152, 9810522367

Preface

The success of agriculture sector depends not only on increase in production, but also on the existence of efficient market and value chain. A common problem faced by farmers, most of which results in unremunerated income for the farmers and thus, perpetual poverty incidence among the farm population. Reorganisation of agriculture market is done in such a way so as to maximise the income of the farmers and can be construed as an effective measure of poverty alleviation. Study on the marketing of agriculture and allied products encompass a broad framework of activities related to value addition and sale of the products. It involves all aspects of market structures, both functional and institutional, based on technical and economic considerations, and includes pre and post-harvest operations, assembling, grading, storage, transportation, and distribution.

Agriculture occupies a prominent place in the economy of the North Eastern Indian state of Mizoram. About 60 per cent of the total workers are engaged in the agriculture and allied sector. Shifting cultivation is the main agricultural practice, while there has been a commendable growth of settled cultivation recently, following the implementation of several government schemes. The state has seen significant progress in cultivated areas for fruits items like orange, pineapple, passion fruit, etc. and had started producing substantial quantities of these fruits. However, in the absence of adequate development in agro-based industries and organised marketing institutions, fruits and vegetables produced in the state are marketed through a network of intermediaries. Unorganised and non-transparent transaction of commodities usually ends in the disadvantage of the producer. Attempt is made in this book to examine the existing marketing practices, channels and stakeholders and the distribution of profit across the value chain of agricultural marketing in Mizoram.

At the outset, I want to express my sincere gratitude to the various market stakeholders in Mizoram, who were interviewed in the process of data collection, for providing us with necessary inputs of this study. The entire exercise would be in vain without their cooperation. The hardship and pain undertaken by the field investigators, who collected the required information from different parts of the state, are given heartfelt acknowledgement and are the architect of this study.

My special thanks go to Mr. Lianhmingthanga, Research Scholar, Department of Economics, Mizoram University, for his untiring support and assistance in the tabulation of field data and proof reading of the manuscript. I am thankful to my wife, Sangpuii, for her constant support and inspiration to go on with this work.

Above all, I thank Almighty God who has showered me with countless blessings, mental faculty, and sound health.

Dated 15.2.2016

James L.T. Thanga
Aizawl

Contents

Abbreviations

AMFU	–	All Mizoram Farmers Union
AMPC	–	Agriculture Produce Market Committee Act
BCAM	–	Brooms Cultivators Association of Mizoram
CDAR	–	Community Development Action and Reflection
DMI	–	Directorate of Marketing and Inspection
FCI	–	Food Corporation of India
GSDP	–	Gross State Domestic Product
HCP	–	Hnamchhantu Pawl
IWDP	–	Integrated Watershed Development Programme
IWMP	–	Integrated Wasteland Management Project
Kg	–	Kilogram
LC	–	Local Council
LCS	–	Land Custom Station
MAHFED	–	Mizoram State Agriculture, Horticulture and Marketing Cooperative Federation Limited
MAMCO	–	Mizoram Agriculture Marketing Corporation Limited
MASCOS	–	Mizoram Sericulture Farming Cooperative Society Limited
MICLUN	–	Mizoram Cultivator and Labour Union
MIFCO	–	Mizoram Food and Allied Industries Corporation Limited
MIGA	–	Mizoram Iskut Grower Association
MIS	–	Market Information System
MIZOFED	–	Mizoram State Cooperative Marketing and Consumer Federation Limited
MPZA	–	Mizo Panhnah Zuar Association
MT	–	Metric Tonnes
MTZA	–	Mahni Thlai Zuar Association
MULCO	–	Mizoram Multi-Commodity Producer Cooperative Union Limited
NGO	–	Non-Governmental Organisation
NLUP	–	New Land Use Policy
NSDP	–	Net State Domestic Product

PDS	–	Public Distribution System
PIGFED	–	Mizoram Pig Producers Cooperative Federation Limited
RPA	–	Rubber Planters Association
SHG	–	Self Help Group
TRIFED	–	Tribal Cooperative Marketing Development Federation of India Limited
T&C	–	Trade and Commerce
VC	–	Village Council
ZAGS	–	Zo-Anthurium Growers Society
ZEP	–	Zopar Export Private Limited
ZOFISFED	–	Mizoram Cooperative Fish Farming, Marketing and Processing Federation Limited

List of Tables and Figures

LIST OF TABLES

LIST OF FIGURES

1

Introduction

Agricultural marketing deals with all the activities, agencies, and policies involved in the procurement of farm inputs by farmers and the movement of agricultural products from farms to consumers (Kakaty & Borah, 2011). It involves all aspects of market structures, both functional and institutional, based on technical and economic considerations, and includes pre and post-harvest operations, assembling, grading, storage, transportation, and distribution. It is general understanding that production and marketing must go hand in hand and that an efficient system of agriculture marketing promotes the expansion of production and cultivated area. However, a common problem faced by most of the underdeveloped, agrarian economies is lack of efficient and organised network of agriculture marketing, which results in perpetual poverty incidence among the farm population. This poverty incidence would persist until the emergence of well organised and efficient marketing channels for agricultural produce in the country.

Agriculture occupies a prominent place in the economy of Mizoram. As per the Economic Classification of Workers in 2001 Census, about 60 per cent of the total workers are engaged in the agriculture and allied sector. In the absence of adequate development in other sectors such as agro-based industries and other industries, it continues to be the main occupation of the people till today. Shifting cultivation (Jhumming) continues to be the prevalent method of cultivation. Both the state and central governments have shown efforts to increase the state's produce and had introduced settled cultivation of agriculture and allied crops as an alternative to the practice of Jhum cultivation. The most prominent scheme introduced in the state is the state's flagship programme of New Land Use Policy (NLUP) since 2010-11 fiscal. Under this scheme, farmers are given assistance for their cultivation in the form of planting materials, finance, etc. Moreover, several centrally sponsored schemes like Integrated Watershed Development Programme (IWDP), Integrated Wasteland Management Project (IWMP), etc. and other state projects like Minor Irrigation Projects were implemented prior to NLUP and are continued till date.

All these efforts have strong impacts on the scenario of agricultural land use and cropping pattern of the state. The distribution of NLUP beneficiaries trade-wise clearly indicates such condition. For example, the number of families who started undertaking orange cultivation during 2010-11 was 4396, which was added to by more than 4000 families during 2011-12. The same trend was also observed in other activities. It is expected that there would be a substantial increase in the state's production of agriculture and allied commodities in the near future. Considering the existing trends, it has become a high time to study the existing scenario of agriculture marketing and initiate a more effective strategy for these commodities.

The state government classified various agricultural and allied crops under different departments namely Agriculture, Horticulture, Soil and Water Conservation, Fisheries, Environment and Forest, and Animal Husbandry. Though, they are officially reported separately in each of these sectors, for simplicity and easier analysis, this study considered the products of all these sectors as agriculture and allied products.

A Brief Profile of Mizoram

The state of Mizoram lies in the North-Eastern part of India, between Latitude 21°58′ and 24°35′ North and Longitude 92°15′Eand93°29′East. It is sandwiched between Myanmar in the East with 404 km long border and, South and Bangladesh in the West with 318 km long border. It is a land-locked state with a total area of 21,087 sq.km. Mizoram is bounded by the states of Assam and Manipur in the North and Tripura in the West. Its topography consists predominantly of mountainous terrain of tertiary rocks. The mountain ranges run in a north to south direction in parallel series. These ranges are separated from one another by narrow and deep river valleys with only few and small patches of flat lands in between them. The terrain of Mizoram is young and so the geomorphic features do not show much diversity in the formation of the landforms. Most of the landforms are erosive in nature.

The drainage system of the state consists of a number of rivers and streams. Most of them are of ephemeral nature, depending on monsoon rains. Their volume and level fluctuate greatly in dry and rainy seasons. Most of the drainage lines originate from the central part of the state and flow towards either north or south influenced by the north-south trending ridge. The main rivers of the state are Tlawng, Tuirial, Tuivawl - all flowing north-wards, and Tiau, Chhimtuipui, Khawtlangtuipui- all flowing south-wards. Mizoram enjoys a pleasant climate, which is neither too hot nor too cold, throughout the year. The summer temperature ranges from 15°C to 29°C, while it is 18°C to 27°C in autumn and 8°C to 25°C in winter. The average rainfall is about 200 cm per year, though it may amount to 350 cm in the northwest part of the state. It generally rains during May to September; July and August being the rainiest month. November to January is a dry period with minimum rainfall.

The majority of the population in Mizoram are Mizowho belong to the Mongoloid stock. From the record of the Population Census 2011, the state's population stood at 10,91,014 with a density of 52 persons per sq. km. The sex ratio is 975 females per 1000 males. There are 8 admininltrative districts in the state namely Aizawl, Lunglei, Saiha, Lawngtlai, Champhai, Serchhip, Kolasib, and Mamit. Aizawl District has the largest population (37.03 per cent of the total population) and Saiha District has the lowest (5.16 percent). Further, majority of the people in the state (around 87 percent) are Christians. The literacy rate of the state is 91.33 per cent, which is the third highest in the country.

The economy of the state is mainly agricultural, with minimal industrial activities and a highly inflated and expanding tertiary sector. Public expenditure is the driving force of the state economy. However, the state is highly dependent on resource transfer from the central government although it generates a small amount of internal resources. The per capita income of Mizoram stood at Rs. 60,836 at current price during 2012-13, while the share of agriculture and allied activities in the Net State Domestic Product (NSDP) is 17.05 per cent at current price during 2012-13. Meanwhile, majority of the population i.e. 55.33 per cent are cultivators who are engaged in agricultural activities mostly by practising Jhum cultivation.

Commercialisation of Agriculture

In the pre-colonial state of society, the economy of the Mizo was not monetised. The people were more or less self-sufficient by exploring with intelligence the economic potential of their surroundings. Lack of surplus products and lack of intercourse with the neighbouring areas reduced trade and commerce to a minimum. Even though modern practices of selling and buying were not known to them, some records reveal that they practiced bartering of goods (Zorema 2012). After the First Lushai Expedition of 1871-72, the government set up and renovated four markets or Bazaars operated by traders from Cachar (Assam) and Manipur (*Laldinpuii,2012*). Following are the markets operated by these traders, mostly located along the major rivers:

(i) Tipaimukh Bazaar on River Tuiruang (Barak River)
(ii) Sonai Bazaar on River Tuirial (Sonai River)
(iii) Changsil Bazaar on River Tlawng (Dhaleswari River)
(iv) Tlabung Bazaar at River Khawthlangtuipui (Karnaphuli River)

As stated, trading was initially done through 'barter system' and it was only from 1891 that the British introduced Indian currency in the Lushai Hills. However, even after coming into contact with the outside world and the establishment of frontier markets, the main purchases made by the Lushai Hills from the Bazaars did not go beyond salts, colour yarns, brass vessels, tobacco, small quantities of iron, etc. in exchange for their rubber, cotton, bee-wax, and other forest products. However, agricultural produce, which existed in any form, was not marketed until the latter half of the twentieth century because there simply was no market for it.

The building of infrastructure such as transport, communication, opening of marts, and the spread of education brought about by the British regime created a climate of change and a new outlook in the Mizo society and economy (Zorema, 2012). Following the political disturbances in 1966, there were massive improvements in infrastructural development, particularly on transportation system thereby resulting in greater mobility of goods and farm products for sale from most of the villages. This encouraged the farmers to cultivate cash crops and sell the marketable surplus. With the elevation of the Mizo District Council to the Union Territory status in 1972 and subsequent statehood in 1987, Mizoram underwent a significant change in the occupational structure. Many people in search of employment opportunities migrated to urban areas and engaged themselves in various alternative occupations like wage labour, petty trade, and Government jobs etc. The result of all this development was that monetised economy came into existence in the state resulting in marketing of goods and services including agriculture and allied products. Thus it was only from the late 1980s that the wave of commercialisation of agriculture gained ground in Mizoram.

In the context of Mizoram, commercialisation would mean increasing involvement of the peasantry in the product market, or in other words, the increasing relative importance of cash crops in the peasants' production. The cropping patterns, internal and external trade, and the degree of market integration reflected in the movement of prices between markets are all indicators of commercialisation in one sense or the other (Nair, 1987). Despite the absence of capitalistic development of agriculture in Mizoram, production of commercial crops has multiplied considerably during the last few decades. This happened both in the Jhum and settled cultivation. Table 1.1, which presents the area used for paddy (the staple food) and major commercial crops in Mizoram for the last 5 decades, can be taken as an indication of the trend in commercialisation of agriculture in Mizoram.

It can be observed from Table 1.1 that during the past five decades, there has been a structural change in the cropping pattern of the state agriculture, with commercial crops gaining importance year after year. In 1974-75, the cultivated area under paddy (staple food) was 78.29 percent while the area under commercial crops accounted only 21.71 per cent of the total cultivated land. However, due to a gradual shift from subsistence to a more commercialised economy, there has been a declining trend of the area under paddy

Table 1.1: Percentage Distribution of Area under Paddy and Major Commercial Crops

Year	*Paddy (%)*	*Commercial crops (%)*	*All crops*
1974-75	78.29	21.71	100
1980-81	72.18	27.82	100
1990-91	59.09	40.91	100
2001-02	57.04	42.96	100
2010-11	40.03	59.97	100

Source: (1) Statistical Abstract (various issues) Dept. of Agriculture, Mizoram (2) Economic Survey (various issues), Department of Planning and Programme Implementation Govt. of Mizoram.

with an increasing trend of area under commercial crops. By 2010-11, the area under paddy (rice) accounted only 40.03 per cent of the total cultivated land, which indicates a decline of 38.26 per cent. At the same time, the area under commercial crops increased to 59.97, thereby, showing a significant growth of commercialisation of agriculture in the state.

In addition to the increased monetisation of the state economy, one of the main factors for increase in commercial crops is the geophysical setting of the state. The moderately sloped areas of the state are suitable for horticulture crops which cover about 21 per cent of total geographical area while only 3 per cent of the total area is considered as a viable potential area for cultivation of paddy (NABARD, 2010). The result of this is that farmers have changed their attitude towards the cultivation of cash crops taking into account the availability of market opportunities. This is justified by the gradual increase of the cultivated area under commercial crops in the state.

The chief factors that contributed significantly to the emergence and growth of commercial farming in Mizoram are penetration of market, monetisation, the geophysical conditions, and the massive improvement in transportation due to political disturbance and various public policies of developmental programmes. However, considering the present agricultural marketing system which is associated with considerable degree of market imperfection, one important issue that has emerged is - to what extent the degree and development of commercialisation would bring about change in the agrarian structure of the state economy. At this juncture, we should not overlook the significance of studying the existing system of agriculture marketing and the roles of various institutions for the overall development of the state agriculture.

Major Agriculture and Allied Crops

Agriculture remains the mainstay of the state economy as it is the source of employment for the majority of the total workforce and a significant contributor to the state domestic product. Around 60 per cent of the population is engaged in agriculture even though the cultivable land is extremely limited as 70 per cent of the land is located in the hilly area with more than 35 per cent slope (Thanga, 2014). According to the record of the government, agriculture and allied activities contributed 18.81 per cent to the Gross State Domestic Product (GSDP) in 2011-12. As per the Economic classification of workers of 2001 census, 65.46 per cent of the total workers are engaged in agriculture and its allied sectors. Like other hill areas in North Eastern India, shifting cultivation (Jhumming) continues to be the main cultivation practice, even though people have started moving towards settled cultivation since the 1980s with the initiatives of the State Government. The major agriculture crops are paddy (rice), maize, pulses, oilseeds, sugarcane, and potato, while the major horticulture crops are banana, fruits, squash, vegetables, spices, etc.

Table 1.2 presents the area and production of major agriculture crops in Mizoram for ten years. Rice is widely consumed as staple food in Mizoram. Currently, around 70 per cent of the state's rice is produced through shifting cultivation. Paddy (rice) cultivation occupies the most important position in the state that it covers 39,242 hectares with total production of 77,471 Metric Tonnes (MT) in 2012-13. However, the trend of the data shows the declining importance of paddy in the state agriculture as its area cover and production have recorded a declining trend. The same trend is also found in cases of maize and oilseeds. Meanwhile, the area and production of other crops like pulses, sugarcane, and potato are more or less constant over the years, though there are certain degrees of fluctuations.

Table 1.3 presents the area and production of major horticulture crops in Mizoram since 2008. Most of the horticulture crops presented here are produced from settled cultivation, while

Table 1.2: Area and Production of Major Agricultural Crops in Mizoram

A= Area (Ha), P = Production (MT)

Year	Paddy		Maize		Pulses		Oilseeds		Sugarcane		Potato	
	A	P	A	P	A	P	A	P	A	P	A	P
2003- 04	59196	114630	10481	20282	4892	4313	7532	5478	1393	6174	363	893
2004 – 05	57085	107661	10505	19788	6741	7971	5817	5321	1357	13565	504	2531
2005 – 06	56460	107740	11742	22703	6861	8663	5870	5560	1383	15953	953	3891
2006 – 07	52851	42091	10775	20969	5054	5833	4075	3755	1340	12187	639	1652
2007 – 08	54541	15688	7328	729	5048	2632	8485	748	883	828	330	1158
2008 – 09	51990	68917	9558	9318	3931	3646	3275	2514	1342	13696	269	1569
2009 – 10	47204	66132	8551	11510	3920	6479	2741	2988	1434	12368	285	2235
2010 – 11	40692	67428	9005	13499	3957	6065	3140	3727	1418	7900	431	3699
2011 – 12	38976	75566	6905	8397	3836	5331	2474	2382	1463	7456	409	2868
2012 – 13	39342	77471	6175	8064	3099	3288	2063	2224	1323	6795	286	1440

Source: 'Statistical Abstracts of Mizoram, 2013', Directorate of Eco. and Stats. Govt. of Mizoram.

Table 1.3: Cultivated Areas and Production of Major Horticulture Crops in Mizoram

A = Area (Ha), P = Production (Metric Tonnes)

Crops		*2008-2009*	*2009-2010*	*2010-2011*	*2011-2012*	*2012-2013*
Banana	A	7,220	8,660	10,040	10,090	10,540
	P	66,424	84,810	1,18,600	1,19,060	1,27,530
Local fruits	A	–	–	–	8,840	9,040
	P	–	–	–	19,310	19,890
M. Orange	A	4,087	5,348	6,515	8,360	8,960
	P	10,757	13,265	19,701	22,238	24,100
Lime/Lemon	A	4,176	4,650	4,823	4,850	7,930
	P	5,898	14,940	24,150	24,710	25,140
Pineapple	A	432	430	1,532	2,720	3,000
	P	2,390	2,808	13,590	19,650	21,960
Grape	A	1,172	1,232	1,575	1,880	2,380
	P	9,962	13,736	20,400	24,300	20,800
Papaya	A	817	770	800	850	1,000
	P	4,493	4,985	6,750	18,190	23,100
Squash	A	2,000	2,250	3,500	4,000	4,500
	P	28,200	34,873	56,849	66,500	75,020
Local Vegetables	A	–	–	–	10,220	11,460
	P	–	–	–	8,380	9,620
Bittergourd	A	3,474	3,580	3,715	3,800	3,900
	P	17,370	18,258	19,110	19,570	20,400
Okra	A	2,749	2,500	2,800	2,950	3,050
	P	11,270	10,500	18,710	19,790	20,742
Cabbage	A	2,985	2,400	2,600	2,800	3,020
	P	23,880	21,600	33,569	37,100	40,080
Beans	A	2,250	2,245	2,290	2,310	2,420
	P	4,725	4,850	4,956	5,040	5,320
Brinjal	A	1,884	1,890	2,010	2,100	2,200
	P	12,246	12,096	12,903	13,500	15,620
Tomato	A	620	635	675	700	800
	P	4,960	5,715	6,180	6,420	7,390
Chilli (fresh)	A	7,185	8,700	8,700	–	–
	P	24,429	47,850	47,850	–	–
Chilli (dried)	A	–	–	–	8,900	9,020
	P	–	–	–	9,790	8,208
Ginger	A	9,391	6,200	6,500	7,010	7,280
	P	34,290	31,000	31,950	34,460	28,390
Turmeric	A	9,625	4,500	4,780	5,580	6,050
	P	39,862	22,500	23,970	29,240	22,990

Source: Horticulture Department, Government of Mizoram, 2014.

some items like local vegetables (mustard leaf, pumpkin leaf, etc.), chilli, brinjal, etc. are mostly from shifting cultivation. Although items like ginger and chilli are classified as agriculture crops in Mizoram, they are classified here under horticulture crops for their affinity to other horticulture crops.

Commodities In and Out of Mizoram

Although agriculture remains to be the main livelihood activity of the people of Mizoram, the state is far from being self-sufficient in most of the agriculture and allied commodities. Rice for Public Distribution System (PDS) has been the largest imported item as the state's own production is sufficient for about 3 months only. Since imported rice has a well organised distribution channel, it is excluded in our analysis. The major imported items and their respective quantities and values are presented in Table 1.4. The data in this table are obtained from the record of Trade and Commerce Department (T&C) Check Gate in the State boundary. The figures presented here may be only part of the actual imports and thus, the total quantity may be much higher in reality. It is observed from the table that more than Rs. 190 Crores worth of these 12 items were imported during 2012-13. The major items in terms of quantity are potato, fish, onion, betel leaf, and other vegetable items.

The major items going out of the state and their estimated volume as recorded by the Check Gate of T&C Department are presented in Table 1.5. It is estimated that more than Rs. 91 Crore worth of these commodities were sold outside the state in 2011-12, which reduced to Rs. 49.82 Crore in 2012-13. The main contributor of the export items is ginger, which is mostly produced from Jhum cultivation. However, its price is highly uncertain. Second to ginger are chilli and turmeric which are marketed outside mostly in raw form through a network of unorganised market intermediaries who hail from neighbouring states of Assam and Manipur.

Marketing and Stakeholders: An Overview

(a) Markets: The State's Trade and Commerce (T&C) Department at present manages 22 major markets and 198 markets

Table 1.4: Major Agriculture and Allied Products Imported from Outside Mizoram (Excluding Rice)

Sl. No.	Item	Unit	2011 – 12			2012 – 13		
			Q'ty	Rs./Unit	Amount (Rs. in Crore)	Q'ty	Rs./Unit	Amount (Rs. in Crore)
1.	Vegetables	Qtls.	39,247	3,500	13.74	60,807	4,000	24.32
2.	Potato	Qtls.	59,632	2,500	14.91	74,400	5,000	37.20
3.	Onion	Qtls.	23,372	3,500	8.18	47,050	7,000	32.94
4.	Pineapple	Qtls.	1,877	3,200	0.60	9,174	3,600	3.30
5.	Cattle	No.	1,300	25,000	3.25	1,337	32,000	4.28
6.	Pig	No.	420	20,000	0.84	240	27,000	0.65
7.	Goat	No.	2,137	3,000	0.64	4,913	3,300	1.62
8.	Poultry	Tukrie**	14,271	5,500	7.85	2,623	6,200	1.63
9.	Egg	Box	87,138	1,050	9.15	85,370	1,155	9.86
10.	Fish	Box***	33,091	6,000	19.85	48,157	7,200	34.67
11.	Betel leaf	Tukrie	29,639	4,500	13.34	47,596	5,500	26.18
12.	Betel nuts	Qtls.	43,610	2,500	10.90	39,608	3,500	13.86
	Total				103.25			190.51

Source: Trade and Commerce Department, Government of Mizoram (* MAMCO), 2014.

Note: ** 34kg, ***40kg

Table 1.5: Major Agriculture and Allied Products Going Out from Mizoram State

Sl. No.	Item	Unit	2011 – 12			2012 – 13		
			Q'ty	Rs./Unit	Amount (Rs. in Crore)	Q'ty	Rs./Unit	Amount (Rs. in Crore)
1.	Squash	Qtls.	12874	800.00	1.03	29063	1,000	2.91
2.	Hatkora	Qtls.	9676	2000.00	1.94	43313	3,000	4.33
3.	Orange	Qtls.	6469	3000.00	1.94	7689	7,000	5.38
4.	Ginger*	Qtls.	184045	25 – 35	55.21	90721	15 – 18	14.97
5.	Turmeric*	Qtls.	78790	8 – 10	7.09	67870	8 – 10	6.11
6.	Chilli*	Qtls.	18970	80 – 150	21.82	12475	80 – 150	14.35
7.	Sesame*	Qtsl.	5440	40 – 60	2.72	3547	40 - 60	1.77
	Total				91.75			49.82

Source: Trade and Commerce Department, Government of Mizoram (2014).

Note: *Average price were used to estimate the total value.

indirectly through the Local Councils (LC) and Village Councils (VC). These markets not only provide venues for selling agricultural produce within the state but also employment to a number of people, especially women. Of the total 220 markets, 176 are village markets and roadside markets managed by the respective VCs. For better regulation and proper administration of markets, the Mizoram State Marketing Board was constituted by the Government under the Mizoram State Agricultural Produce Marketing Act 1996. Through this Board, marketing committees were constituted in major markets such as New Market in Aizawl, Vaivakawn Market, Bawngkawn Market, and Vairengte Market. Recently, Government of India formulated the Model Act on Agricultural Marketing for the states for marketing reforms in India. However, the state Act has not been reviewed and amended in conformity with the model Act basically because the markets in Mizoram are relatively small with lesser producers and buyers than other states. As a result, the markets in the State are not well regulated yet.

(b) Trade to/from other States: In order to protect the farmers in Mizoram from unhealthy market competition with middlemen and the like from other states, the Mizoram Agriculture Products (Prohibition of Movement) Bill was enacted in 1999. This Act listed 136 items in which no person is allowed to transport the items to any place beyond and into the state of Mizoram without a permit issued by the State Government or any officers authorised by the government. In this regard, T&C Department has check gate offices in Vairengte (Kolasib District), Bairabi (Kolasib District), Kanhmun (Mamit District), and Mualkawi (Champhai District). The movements of these commodities are, thus, checked and recorded by this Department.

(c) International Trade: The Ministry of Commerce and Industry, Government of India appointed T&C Department as the nodal department for the promotion of border trade with the neighbouring countries—Myanmar and Bangladesh. Three international trade gates are proposed along the international boundary. They are Zokhawthar (Champhai District) for Indo-Myanmar trade; Kawrpuichhuah (Tlabung, Lunglei District) for Indo-Bangladesh trade; and Zorinpui (Lawngtlai District) for Indo-Myanmar trade. Of these trade points, Zokhawthar has already been officially commissioned. At present, 62 items of commodities are allowed for export and import trading by the Directorate General of Foreign Trade, Government of India.

(d) Marketing Agents: Based on the field survey, the main marketing agents operating in Mizoram can be broadly classified into four. These agents and their characteristics are presented in Table 1.6.

Table 1.6: Characteristics of Major Marketing Stakeholders in Mizoram

Stakeholders	*Characteristics*
Producers	Generally, they sell their produce to collectors or wholesale agents who come to their villages. At the same time, some producers transport their produce to markets located in towns/cities and sell them directly to consumers or retailers (vendors)
Wholesalers/ Wholesale Commission Agents	They are the traders who collect or procure the commodities from the producers and sell it in bulk to the retailers who would further sell the commodities to the consumers. They or their agents would go to different parts of the state to collect vegetables from farmers and then sell them to retailers in the nearby town/city market places. Members of Mahni Thlai Zuar Association (MTZA), own produce vegetable marketing association, are the main actors. Although members of MTZA declare themselves to be farmers, they, in fact, act as wholesalers or as a link between producers and retailers.
Collectors/ Commission Agents	They are marketing agents who act as a link between producers and wholesalers or retailers. They earn profit in the process of collection, storage, transportation, and distribution of commodities. It may be noted that there are individuals in the villages who collect surplus produce of vegetables in their respective villages for onward delivery to the wholesale dealers. At the same time, some well-to-do families of the village or from other villages, who have transport vehicles, collect these commodities from the villages, transport and then sell them to retailers operating in urban areas at the prevailing wholesale prices, thus, earning certain amount of profits in the chain. These agents are also considered as collectors.
Retailers	They are the marketing agents who are in direct contact with consumers. There are some instances where wholesalers are also involved in selling commodities directly to consumers. Similarly, the producers are also selling their produce directly to consumers by retailing it at certain marketing areas. It is a common practice to market the products through any of the abovementioned channels.

Source: Market Survey, December 2013 – March 2014.

The Study and Methodology

The main objective is to examine the existing status of agriculture marketing in Mizoram, on the basis of the marketing of selected agricultural commodities. The key objectives of the study are as follows:

1. To study the marketing channels of various agricultural products in Mizoram.
2. To study the various marketing stakeholders of the selected commodities and value chain of the distribution flow indicating cost and margin structure of the stakeholders involved.
3. To examine seasonal conditions such as peak and off seasons for quantity arrivals and the related cost fluctuations.

It also studies the existing conditions of physical and institutional infrastructure for agriculture marketing and presents the role of some public and private marketing institutions in the state.

Survey Coverage and Period: It covers 20 selected agriculture and allied commodities in Mizoram. Marketing aspect of these selected commodities were examined and studied on the basis of the information obtained from field survey. The items considered are as follows:

1. Mustard Leaf	2. Cabbage	3. Fish
4. Bean	5. Brinjal	6. Green Chilli
7. Pineapple	8. Potato	9. Banana
10. Tomato	11. Onion	12. Garlic
13. Lemon	14. Ginger	15. Orange
16. Squash	17. Turmeric	18. Areca-nut
19. Broom	20. Anthurium flower	

Field work was conducted during the period of November 2013 to January 2014. Since the survey period was off-season for some of the commodities (e.g. pineapple), the required information was obtained from the retailers and wholesalers according to their recollection only as traders selling of the above commodities hardly kept proper records of their activities in respect to prices, sources and quantity arrivals, even for a few days.

Data: Data was collected from two broad sources: primary and secondary. The former was collected through sample survey, while the latter from secondary sources of information. They are given in detail below:

Sample Design: Purposive sampling strategy was adopted to collect the required data in this survey. This is due to the fact that an adoption of simple random techniques calls for the possibility of selecting some market agents who are not or had never been involved in the commodities of interest. So, the representative marketing agents who are actually dealing with the selected commodities were included in the sample. Since the use of uniform questionnaires was later found infeasible to evaluate the required information, interview method was adopted for the entire survey.

To capture the marketing channels and chain management of the selected items, data was collected from three broad sources, namely, retailers/vendors, wholesalers/middlemen, and facilitator associations/societies. Sample of retail sellers (vendors) were selected from different market places located in Aizawl, Seling, Champhai, Serchhip and Lunglei. These agents are an important link between the producers, wholesalers, and consumers and hence, information obtained from them is very crucial in our analysis. Various stakeholders covered in the field survey are given in Table 1.7.

The retail vendors had difficulty in furnishing detailed information regarding the sources, prices, origin, etc. of the items they sell. It is, thus, rather difficult to ascertain the actual marketing channel from these agents who simply bought the vegetables from the wholesale dealers (or commission agents) at the prevailing rate and sell it to the consumers without any enquiry of the origin and other stakeholders. Movement of commodities from producers to wholesalers was also observed. To this end, various NGOs and associations that are directly or indirectly involved in the marketing of the specified commodities were interviewed. Some of these organisations function as facilitator organisations; while some are operating like that of trading organisations/ establishments. The NGOs covered in the survey are mentioned below.

Table 1.7: List of Various Stakeholders in the Market Survey

Sl. No.	*Stakeholders*	*Level*	*Hqtrs.*	*Main Activities*	*Area Represented*
1.	Mahni Thlai Zuar Association (MTZA)	State level NGO	Aizawl New Market	Coordination and Facilitation of Wholesale Marketing; members' welfare	Mizoram
2.	Vegetables Seller Associations	NGOs in each market	Bazaar	Members Welfare and pricing regulations	In each Bazar/Market
3.	Mizoram Iskut Growers Association (MIGA)	State Level NGO	Sihphir	Facilitation of Squash Market and members' Welfare	Villages in and around Siphir area
4.	Ginger Growers Association - 6 nos	Village Level NGO	–	Welfare of the Ginger Growers	Ruallung, Mualpheng, Rulchawm, Sateek, Tachhip and Thiak
5.	Kuhva Ching Association (Arecanut Growers Association) - 2 no	Village Level NGO	–	Welfare of the Growers	Bilkhawthlir and Zamuang
6.	Hnamchhantu Pawl	State Level	Aizawl	Procurement, Processing and marketing of Brooms	Mizoram
7.	Zopar Export Private Limited (ZEP)	All India Level marketing Company	Bangalore	Marketing of Anthurium in domestic and international market	India
8.	Zo-Anthurium Growers Society (ZAGS)	State Level Society	Aizawl	Marketing and Procurement of Anthurium Flowers	Mizoram

(*Contd.*)

Sl. No.	Stakeholders	Level	Hqtrs.	Main Activities	Area Represented
9.	Sangha Dil Nei Association (Fish Farmers Associaiton)	Village Level NGO	–	Marketing of locally produced fish	Bilkhawthlir area
10.	Individuals	1. 43 vegetable and fruit retailers in different market stations 2. 2 successful growers of arecanut each in Zamuang and Bilkhawthlir villages 3. 8 wholesale dealers of vegetables 4. 6 commission agents for fish 5. 18 wholesalers of potato, onion, garlic and turmeric powder. 6. 2 retailers of flowers in Aizawl			

First, members of farm community who organised themselves as wholesalers by procuring vegetables from the producers and sell it to the retailers, in the name of association of own produce sellers called 'Mahni Thlai Zuar Association (MTZA)', were interviewed. MTZA has more than 400 members who hail from different parts of the state. They hold regular meetings within the premises of Aizawl New Market. Members of this association are normally farmers who collect the locally produced vegetables from different parts of the state, in addition to their own products, and sell them in bulk to the retailers/vendors in different market places at wholesale prices. The MTZA is known to have a strong influence on the prices of vegetables being marketed in the state.

Second, representatives of different growers associations for the selected products were also interviewed. The main objectives of these organisations are to promote mutual harmony among the growers/members and to protect them from adverse effects of open price competition. Organisations covered in the field survey are: Mizoram Iskut (Squash) Grower Association (MIGA); ginger growers associations in six villages of Mualpheng, Ruallung, Rulchawm, Sateek, Tachhip, and Thiak; Kuhva Ching Association (Arecanut Growers Association) in Bilkhawthlir and Zamuang villages; Sangha Khawitu Association (Fish Farmers Association), Bilkhawthlir; and vegetable sellers associations in different market places. These associations keep a record of the activities of their members in respect to prices, quantity arrivals, and other relevant information, as far as possible.

Third, there are some organisations which help or facilitate the farmers in the marketing of their products. Such organisations covered in the field survey are Hnamchhantu Pawl (HCP), Zo-Anthurium Growers Society (ZAGS), and Zopar Export Private Limited (ZEP). Lastly, it was found that there were associations of vegetable sellers in each market covered in the field work. These associations regulate the activities of their member sellers in respect to pricing of the produce and at the same time, take initiatives for their welfare.

Secondary Data: Secondary data were obtained from various published and unpublished reports of the state government, NGOs, and other marketing agents. Published official records were mostly obtained from various issues of Statistical Handbook of Mizoram published by Directorate of Economics and Statistics, Economic

Survey of Mizoram published from time to time by Planning and Programme Implementation Department, Citizens' Charter by Trade and Commerce Department, and Reports and Manuals of Government Departments and their agencies. Information was also obtained from the records of some marketing agencies like *Hnamchhantu Pawl (HCP), Zopar Export Private Limited (ZEP), Mizoram Iskut Growers Association (MIGA), Zo-Anthurium Growers Society (ZAGS),* etc. The information obtained from these sources were analysed and processed to suit the needs of the study.

2

Institutional Set Up of Agriculture Marketing in Mizoram

The presence of an efficient physical and institutional infrastructure in the country would be beneficial for the producers as well as the final consumers. Due to lack of efficient physical infrastructure in many underdeveloped countries, the presence of a network of organised marketing institutions is highly crucial to ensure smooth flow of commodities from producers to final consumers. In spite of the fact that Mizoram has been an agrarian state since time immemorial and had started commercialising its agricultural produce from the last few decades, there is no sufficient marketing infrastructure in place to cope with the growing marketable surplus. As Mizoram had not implemented the Agriculture Produce Market Committee Act (APMC), there is no *mandis*like organised institution that facilitate agriculture marketing. Consequently, the farmers depend on the unorganised networks of intermediaries to market their produce. So, the emergence of an efficient institution that would reorganise the existing agriculture marketing system should be one of the key necessities for agriculture development in Mizoram.

The Concept of Market Regulations and its Evolution in Mizoram

Under traditional system of agriculture marketing, the producers themselves are the sellers (producer-sellers) who had to incur marketing cost and suffer from unscrupulous deductions of charges and malpractices in the system. To ensure orderly marketing and to create fair competition with enhanced bargaining power of the producers-sellers (farmers), public intervention to exercise control of the market with statutory authority is necessary. Thus, the need for the emergence of a regulated market is felt at various levels of the society.

Regulated market aims at the elimination of unhealthy and unscrupulous practices, reduction in marketing charges, and the provision of facilities to the producer-sellers in the market. Any legislative measure designed to regulate the marketing of agricultural produce to establish, improve, and enforce standard marketing practices and charges may be termed as one which aims at the establishment of regulated market. Regulated markets are established by State Government with established rules and regulations for the smooth conduct of business. The basic objective is to create conditions for efficient performance of private trade through the facilitation of free and informal competition. Therefore, a farmer is able to sell his marketed surplus in the presence of several buyers through open and competitive bidding. The legislation for its establishment usually does not mandate the farmer to sell his produce in the regulated market yard only; rather, voluntary action on the part of the farmers is envisioned.

In India, the need for the regulation of markets was felt by the British rulers to ensure availability of supplies of pure cotton at reasonable prices to textiles mills in Manchester (UK). The first regulated market, named *Karanjia Cotton Market,* was established in 1886 under the Hyderabad Residency Order. The first legislation was the Berar Cotton and Grain Market Act of 1897. Under the provision of this Act, the British Resident acquired the authority to declare any place in an assigned district the market for sale and purchase of agricultural produce, and to form a committee to supervise the regulated markets. Regulation of market for agricultural products was emphasised by several committees and commissions from time to time.

In independent India, Mizoram (then Lushai Hills) continued to be one of the districts of Assam. With the establishment of the Mizo District Council in 1952, the responsibility of maintaining and regulating the market system was entrusted to the Council. Pursuant to Paragraph 11 of the Sixth Schedule of the Constitution of India, the Mizo District Council passed a regulation for the management and control of markets to be operative in its jurisdiction. It was named "The Mizoram District (Market)

Regulation 1954" and "The Mizo District (Market) Rules 1956". After this, all markets within Mizoram came under the government control. The rules and regulation were in force till 1996 when it was repealed.

In any case, the rules were not effectively enforced to regulate marketing of ginger, chilli, squash etc. as the Rules are apparently short of the required legal backing though it dealt with the management and control of market—which is considered a crucial matter (Lawmthanga, 1997). Since this is the case, the concerned officials were unable to check various undesirable activities of few traders who were believed to be exerting united efforts to offer the farmers the lowest possible prices for their produce on one pretext or the other (Zonuntluanga, 2002). Thus for the better regulation, establishment, and proper administration of agriculture market in the state, "The Mizoram State Agricultural Produce Marketing (Regulation) Act, 1996" and "The Mizoram State Agricultural Produce Marketing Regulation (General) Rules, 1996" were legislated in 1996 which came into force immediately.

Although the two rules provide some improvement in the arrangement of internal markets, they are hardly sufficient to ensure an orderly conduct for marketing of farm products like ginger, turmeric, chilli, squash, sesame etc. exported and sold outside. Thus, it was later restructured to conform to the Model Act framed by the Government of India and hence, "The Mizoram State Agricultural Produce Marketing (Development and Regulation) Act 2008" was passed in 2008. Unfortunately, the Act could not be implemented due to lack of supporting rules to be notified in the Official Gazette as required by Chapter-I Rule 1(3) of the Act.

The task of management and control of market (including agricultural marketing) was entrusted to such statutory institutions as Land Revenue and Settlement Department, Local Administration Department, Agriculture Department, and Village Councils in their respective jurisdiction. The full economic potential of these markets could not be realised as the system has to cope with the dictates of different entities which have conflicting views at times. To remove this duplicity, the management and administration of markets within the state have now been exclusively placed under the Trade and Commerce Department as per the provision of "The Government of Mizoram (Allocation of Business) Rules 1987". Agricultural marketing is kept under the Trade and Commerce Department and its sponsored agency Mizoram Agriculture Marketing Corporation Limited (MAMCO), which used to be shouldered by the market wing of the same, since 1997. In spite of this demarcation, the Trade and Commerce Department and MAMCO Ltd are practically taking care of the exported (to other states) crops like ginger, chilli, squash, cotton, sesame, while marketing of farm and non-farm products at the periodic markets are still at the hands of Revenue and Local Administration Department till date.

Marketing Infrastructures

The availability of marketing infrastructure affects the structure, conduct, and performance of the market. In the context of agriculture, adequate marketing infrastructures are considered to be one of the most important indicators of agricultural development as they provide basic supportive market amenities and facilities which are conducive for efficient agricultural marketing. Agriculture marketing infrastructure refers to a collection of various facilities, both physical and institutional, that promote trading of agricultural commodities. It includes all amenities and facilities required for the smooth functioning of agricultural marketing system and, at the same time, increase marketing efficiency resulting in better market price for the products. It includes physical infrastructure like agricultural produce market, transport, processing, grading and standardisation, storage, market information system (MIS), communication, finance, post-harvest technology, market education, research, and training. The existing status of Mizoram in the provision of some of the key market infrastructures for agricultural produces may be outlined as follows:

(a) Agricultural Produce Market

Regulated market and market yard are yet to emerge in the state. At present, the only form of market available to the farmer-sellers to dispose-off their products is periodic market. Presently, there are 220 markets (periodic, wholesale, and rural primary markets) directly or indirectly under the control of the state's T&C

Department. As the number is small considering the increasing need of the farmers, selling of vegetables and other agricultural crops along roadside by hawkers has emerged in different parts of the state, particularly in the urban areas.

Most of the existing periodic markets in Mizoram are not commodity specific. They are rather typical rural haats (market) catering to daily requirements, both agriculture and non-agriculture, of the local people. These markets are retail in nature except bi-weekly market at Vairengte, daily Aizawl Market, and Lunglei Super Market which have a mixture of both retail and wholesale trade. They lack even the minimum infrastructure facilities. Very few markets have toilets or water supply. Facilities like storage, packing, grading, garbage disposal etc. are almost non-existent. Auctioning and bidding system are absent in these markets. The only method of sale in all the markets is mutual negotiations resulting in un-remunerative price for the farmers and even the retail sellers. Following the absence of regulated market and the inadequacy of existing markets to handle and serve the required distributional purpose of various crops in large volume, like ginger, chilli, squash, turmeric etc., almost all the marketed surplus of these commodities is disposed of to wholesale market outside the state through the floating traders, local agents, or itinerants dealers.

(b) Grading and Standardization

Standardisation is the process of fixing certain norms for the products that are established by customs or traditions or by a certain authority. It involves determination of basic characteristics of a product on the basis of which the product can be divided into various groups. It also means determining the standards of products with regard to size, colour form, weight, shape, and quality. Grading, on the other hand, is a physical process and involves division of products into classes made up of units possessing similar characteristics. Proper grading and standardisation not only improve the quality but also reduce wastage, attracts buyers, and ensure better prices for agricultural produce. Grading of agricultural produce induces farmers to grow quality products on the one hand, and on the other, the buyers find no difficulty in identifying a suitable one for paying the right price. Categorisation of agricultural produce into different grades would make testing easy to its purity. Grading and Standardization, therefore, not only enable the farmers to give a guarantee of its quality to buyers but also ensure relatively better prices for their produce.

Recognising the significance of grading and standardisation, the Government of India passed the Agricultural Produce (Grading and Marketing) Act way back in 1937. The Directorate of Marketing and Inspection (DMI) was the nodal department to implement the Act and goes under the name of trademark as "AGMARK." The department has a framed Agmark Grade specification for different commodities and also specially framed "Commercial Grade" at the producer level grading. The programme was implemented through the state marketing Department in collaboration with the Marketing boards, Marketing cooperatives, and Marketing committees. The system simplifies the procedure of sale and purchase of agricultural commodities and at the same time ensures the price of the products and quality goods to the buyer.

There is no Agmark Laboratory and commercial grading centre in Mizoram. The farmers simply adopt their own standard of grading, and hence they cannot get remunerative price for their products. Majority of farmers dispose-off their products in ungraded form which results in their inability to identify the prices for different grades/varieties for various cash crops. It is, therefore, imperative for policy makers to establish facilitative infrastructures which would promote the emergence of grading activity of farm products.

(c) Processing

The level of processing capacity is one of the most important parameter for methodical agriculture marketing system. A strong and efficient agro-processing unit requires huge raw materials and consumes farm products on a large scale. It serves as an important market for the farmers/sellers to dispose their products. Since the price of processed products is more stable to great extent, a processing unit can assure stable procurement price for the products, thereby preventing farmers from the risk of price fluctuations. Further, processing of commodities ensure value addition and generate employment opportunities in its operation.

Like other North Eastern states, Mizoram is still backward in agro-processing industry. The major agro-processing units established in Mizoram, all are under Public Sector, till today are as follows:

(i) Food Preservation Factory at Vairengte with a capacity of 1 tonne per day for canning of bamboo shoots and *baibing*, and processing of orange, pineapple etc.
(ii) Spices Processing Plant at Sairang for processing of turmeric, ginger, chilli etc.
(iii) Maize Milling Plant at Khawzawl.
(iv) Food Process Plant at Sairang to process orange, pineapple, passion fruit etc.
(v) Fruit Juice Concentration Plant at Chhingchhip.
(vi) Central processing unit at Sairang to process crops like turmeric, ginger, chillies, fruits and other horticultural products.
(vii) Broom processing unit at Seling.
(viii) Drying Machine for ginger and chillies at Tuirial with a capacity to dry 500 kgs of these items per day.
(ix) Tea processing units at Ngopa and Biate.

It is reported that the working and operation of these processing units are well below the capacity to meet the requirement of the state. In fact, many of them are un-operational and defunct. This may be due to inadequate and irregular supply of raw-materials, old and inefficient equipment, poor management, and lack of proper work plan. Further, due to the seasonal nature of business and lack of proper support from the government, many private players shy away from investing in the sector. Thus, the state has experienced post-harvest losses multiple times for most of the cash crops such as ginger, chilli, squash, turmeric, etc. This further necessitated selling the crops in raw form for which farmers have to rush their sale resulting in low returns in most of the cases.

(d) Warehouse and Storage Facilities

A warehouse in its broad sense is a godown where goods are stored in between its movement from producers' hand to the places of processing and final consumption. Warehouse and storage facilities are important aspects of agricultural marketing facilitating the producer, middlemen, manufacturers, and consumers to achieve the desired standard of trading and disposal. The benefits that the warehouse and storage facilities provide can be summarised as follows:

(i) They give farmers an increase in bargaining power and help them secure better price of their produce.
(ii) They tend to regulate price fluctuations and stabilises price as it equates supply to demand.
(iii) They facilitate future trading.
(iv) They occupy an important place in implementing the agricultural price policy of the government.
(v) They minimised huge wastage which occurs from improper storage of agricultural produce.
(vi) They render various subsidiary services viz. sorting and packaging commodities for shipment, cleaning and drying commodities, acting as forwarding agents for exporters, collecting and disseminating market intelligence.

In 1944, the Reserve Bank of India recommended that every State Government should build warehouses and regulate the system of storage. Again in 1954, the All India Rural Credit Survey Committee recommended warehouses be build and that they should be a part of rural credit and marketing. It recommended a three-tier storage system at (i) National level (ii) State and District Level (iii) Village and rural level (*Sahoo,2011*). As a result of the recommendation, the government passed an Act called Agricultural Produce (Development and Warehousing) Corporation Act in 1956, which was further separated in 1962 into two parts, National Cooperative Development Corporation Act 1962 and the Warehousing Corporation Act of 1962. These Acts mandated both the centre and state to have warehousing corporation. Accordingly, The National Cooperative Development Corporation, The Central Warehousing Corporation, and the State Warehousing Corporation in each state came into existence and many warehouses and storage facilities were constructed both at the national and state level. It should be noted that the storage and warehouse facilities of both the central and state warehousing corporations are mostly utilised by the Food Corporation of India, traders for stocking rice and fertilisers, while a very small fraction of the storage capacity is utilised by farmers. These principal agencies have therefore, by and large, tended to bypass the requirement of the farming community in the rural sector (*Behari, 1992*).

In Mizoram, the central and state warehousing corporation and the cooperative department have not made commendable achievements. Up to March 2010, there are 144 godowns and warehouses (both pucca and semi-pucca) with a storage capacity of 37,330 MT (Table 4.2). Food Corporation of India (FCI) also has 6 Storage Depot with a storage capacity of 22,900 MT. However, these godowns and warehouses are not in consonance with the requirement of the farm population (Vanrammawia, 2015). Besides these, most of the rural godowns constructed by the cooperative department/government are located far away from the villages and have no caretakers/keepers attached to them. Thus, they are hardly being used since they are not free from the attack of rodents, insects, damp, and thief.

Due to inadequate availability of warehouses and storage facilities, not to speak of cold storage facilities, the farmers of Mizoram are compelled to sell their produce immediately after harvest to prospective buyers earning un-remunerative price at the nearest road-head or villages as and when the buyer find it worthwhile to come. There was no cold storage facility functioning in the state till the new multi-chambered cold storage was inaugurated on 10th February, 2007 at Vairengte. It should be noted that cold storage facilities preserve the agricultural goods for longer period and protect them from deterioration of their quality. The cold storage established in 2007 was expected to cater the need for judicious storage of varied essential commodities like potato, chilli, turmeric, squash, and ginger. Unfortunately, it was non-functional immediately after, mostly due to failure in management and lack of political will for its continuation, and hence, it is now on the verge of closing down. Table 2.1 presents the existing number of storage godowns in Mizoram.

(e) Market Information System (MIS)

The availability of reliable information about market on quantity arrival, prices, etc. improve the decision-making capacity of the

Table 2.1: Godowns and Warehouses in Mizoram (up to March 2010)

Sl.	*District*	*Pucca*	*Semi- Pucca*	*Total*	*Storage Capacity (in MT)*
1.	Mamit	2	15	17	3910
2.	Kolasib	2	8	10	2550
3.	Aizawl	3	27	30	7450
4.	Champhai	4	23	27	6170
5.	Serchhip	2	13	15	3850
6.	Lunglei	0	14	14	5400
7.	Lawngtlai	1	7	8	3050
8.	Saiha	1	22	23	4950
	Total	15	129	144	37330

Source: Statistical Handbook Mizoram, 2010, Directorate of Economics and statistics.

farmers and strengthen their bargaining power. Market information service in India is mainly confined to collection of data on prices and arrivals of commodities from certain important assembling or regulated market. Due to the absence of regulated market in Mizoram, the working of market information system is far from satisfactory. The Directorate of Economics and Statistics, Government of Mizoram collects farm harvest price and publishes it for public knowledge from time to time. However, this hardly sufficed the requirement of the farm communities as it normally fails to provide the prevailing price in the wholesale and terminal market. In fact, the producers-sellers have to depend on verbal information they obtained from local commission agent or their neighbourhood about market conditions, market arrivals, demand condition, ruling prices, market trend, etc. Lack of sufficient MIS results in market imperfection of various forms in the state. The farmers are, therefore, left with no alternative but to dispose-off their produce in the nearest market or village even at uneconomic prices quoted by private traders.

(f) Marketing Inspection, Research and Training

The efficient working of marketing inspection, research and training improves the know-how and decision making power of the farmers as to when, where, and in what form to sell their produce. There is a dire need to make adequate arrangements for marketing, education, research extension, market inspection, and occasional survey of market which will go a long way to help in identifying problems and finding solutions for efficient marketing system. The need to investigate marketing methods, changing demand, cost, and prices is no less significant. Similarly, marketing personnel need to be oriented to the marketing needs of the farmers.

At the national level, the government has paid attention to these requirements. The Directorate of Marketing and Inspection (DMI) undertakes inspection of major agricultural products throughout the country. The Directorate also undertakes research in various marketing problems. In Mizoram, however, the performance of various institutions and concerned departments viz. Directorate of Agriculture, Directorate of Horticulture, Directorate of Trade and Commerce, MAMCO Ltd. are rather below expected. They cannot deliver services needed by the farmers and market functionaries to tackle their marketing problems. There is no research institution worth mentioning that specialises in agricultural marketing.

Roles of Existing Marketing Institutions

The existing agriculture marketing institutions of the state can be broadly divided into four, namely state institutions, private institutions, agriculture cooperative societies and associations. Each of these bodies are further divided into a number of segments depending on their basic purposes and activities. For example, NGO/Association can take the form of vegetable sellers associations, growers (cum marketing) association, wholesale dealers association, etc. Figure 2.1 presents an organisational outline of these institutions.

State Institutions

Public intervention in commodity marketing is an ingredient to protect the interest of various sections of the society, namely farmers, businessmen, consumers, etc. This is more important for agricultural produce marketing because farmers are often exploited by traders and middlemen. Recognising this fact, Mizoram state government had also attempted to regulate commodity markets in the state. Earlier, the task of regulating

Figure 2.1: Organizational Chart of Agricultural Marketing Institutions in Mizoram

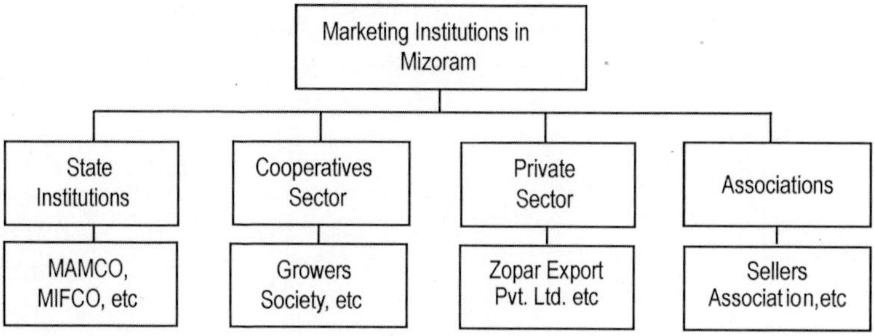

agricultural commodity market was entrusted to the Marketing Wing of the state's Agriculture Department until it was transferred to the Trade and Commerce (T&C) Department in 1997. At the same time, the state government also instituted public corporations during the 1990s that undertake initiatives of marketing agricultural products. The state institutions that are at work for the marketing of agricultural commodities are given as follows:

(a) Trade and Commerce Department

Trade and Commerce (T&C) Department was established by an Act of the State Legislature in 1987. As per the Amendment of this Act in 2007, the department was assigned the responsibilities of promoting and regulating trade and commerce, border trade, agriculture marketing, provision of marketing infrastructure, etc. in the state. It has district offices in Lunglei, Champhai, and Kolasib in addition to its Directorate in Aizawl. It is presently manned by a total of 159 staff.

The department gives priority to improve the marketing aspect of agricultural produce by providing physical market infrastructure to protect the general interest of the farmers (T&C Dept., 2012). Its main activities with respect to trading regulation in the state are issuing permit/pass/license to traders for commodities notified under Mizoram Trading Regulation; monitoring commodity movement beyond and into the state by putting in place check-gates in 4 places, namely Vairengte (Kolasib District), Kanhmun (Mamit District), Bairabi (Kolasib District), and Mualkawi (Champhai District); and collecting stall rents in the market being operated by the department. It may be noted that although the department is authorised to issue permits or license for the movement of agricultural commodities, it is difficult to ascertain to what extent the department had taken up such responsibilities because agricultural produce marketing is still currently characterised by unorganised marketing channels.

With respect to providing market infrastructure, the department directly or indirectly operates as many as 220 markets within the state. These markets not only provide venues for selling agricultural produce within the state, but also employment to a number of people, particularly to women and weaker sections of the society. Moreover, the department was allotted 44 market sites on land lease basis by the state government; with 19 sites in Aizawl district, 8 in Kolasib district, 9 in Lunglei district, 4 in Champhai district, 2 in Mamit district, and 2 in Serchhip district. The department has its own buildings for shops and godowns in various market places are presented in Table 2.2.

Table 2.2: Details of Shops/Godowns Rented Out by Trade and Commerce Department

Sl. No	*Market Place*	*No. of Shops/Godowns*
1.	New Market, Aizawl	290
2.	Vaivakawn Market, Aizawl	8
3.	Bawngkawn Market, Aizawl	10
4.	Bairabi Market, Kolasib District	2
5.	Vairengte Market, Kolasib District	2
6.	Kanhmun Market, Mamit District	11
7.	Lunglei Super Market, Lunglei	151
	Total	474

Source: 'Citizens' Charter 2012', Directorate of Trade and Commerce Department, Govt. of Mizoram.

In addition to provision of shops and godowns rented out in these market places, the department also issues hawker permits in 18 places within the state. These hawkers/vendors have to pay certain amount of fees which is collected by authorised individuals. Usually, these collectors are selected for a period of 6 months through auctioning quotations to be responded to by potential collectors.

Another significant role played by T&C department is its responsibility of promoting border trade between the state and its neighbouring countries of Myanmar and Bangladesh. The department has been appointed as the nodal department by the Ministry of Commerce and Industry, Government of India. The successful implementation of border trade would open access to South-East Asian countries through these two neighbouring countries. Presently, border trade is being proposed at three points.

1. Zokhawthar, Champhai District, for Indo-Myanmar Trade
2. Kawrpuichhuah, Lunglei District, for Indo-Bangladesh Trade
3. Zorinpui, Lawngtlai District, for Indo-Myanmar Trade

Construction of necessary infrastructure for the establishment of Land Custom Station (LCS) for these trade points is underway with financial support from Ministry of Commerce and Industry, Government of India. Of these, all the requirements for the functioning of LCS at Zokhawthar have reportedly been completed and formal commissioning is being awaited. Further, the Director General of Foreign Trade, Government of India permitted export and import of 40 items through this Border Trade Point. As this Point is yet to be formally commissioned by the Central Government, there is no formal trade on the listed items. But even so, informal exchange of commodities has been taking place regularly. The items included for export-import through Zokhawthar Border Trade Point is given in Table 2.3.

Even though the Zokhawthar Point is not yet commissioned to accommodate formal trade between the two countries, informal trade had taken place for many items irrespective of the commodities permitted by the Director General of Foreign Trade. According to Bezbaruah (2009), the estimated volume of informal trade across this point turned out to be more than Rs. 46 crores during 2003-04. The major traded items are textiles and footwear (39.48 percent), livestock (25.47 percent), electrical and electronic items (16.74 percent), and food and beverages (6.44 percent).

(b) Mizoram Agriculture Marketing Corporation (MAMCO) Limited

The Mizoram Agriculture Marketing Corporation Limited (MAMCO Ltd) was instituted as a state undertaking by the Government of Mizoram on 26th February, 1993. The authorised share capital of the corporation is Rs. 10 crores. The main objectives of this corporation are as follows:

Table 2.3: List of Commodities Permitted for Export/Import through Zokhawthar Border Trade Point

1	Mustard/Rape Seed	2	Pulses and beans
3	Fresh Vegetables	4	Fruits
5	Garlic	6	Onion
7	Chillies	8	Spices (excluding Nut Meg, Mace, Cassia and cloves)
9	Bamboo	10	Minor Forest Products (Ex. Teak)
11	Food Items	12	Betel Nuts and Leaves
13	Tobacco	14	Tomato
15	Reed Broom	16	Sesame
17	Resin	18	Coriander Seeds
19	Soya Bean	20	Roasted Sunflower seeds
21	Katha	22	Ginger
23	Bicycle spare parts	24	Life-saving drugs
25	Fertilizer	26	Insecticides
27	Cotton fabrics	28	Stainless steel utensils
29	Menthol	30	Agarbati
31	Spices	32	Cosmetic
33	Leather footwear	34	Paint and Varnishes
35	Sugar and Salt	36	Mosquito Coils
37	Bulb	38	Blades
39	X-ray paper and Photo paper	40	Imitation Jewellery

Source: Trade and Commerce Department, Government of Mizoram.

1. To undertake, assist, finance, and promote business of purchase, sale, storage, processing, export and import of agricultural produce.
2. To render services of all types with or without consideration to the farmers in production and sale of agricultural produce.
3. To provide minimum support price for agriculture produce and also to make commercial purchases and sales.
4. To promote or conduct any commercial or industrial enterprise establishment or company of concern for agricultural produce.

Though the operational scope of MAMCO Ltd. is extended to all products of agriculture, horticulture, animal husbandry, piggery, fishery, forest, and sericulture, it is engaged in the marketing of 8 major cash crops of the state. They are ginger, chilli, sesame, turmeric, squash, orange, hatkora, and tung. It was authorised to issue permit for the movement of these products beyond the state of Mizoram. Later, the government of Mizoram declared this corporation as the state government authorised nodal agency for marketing ginger, chilli, sesame, cotton, and turmeric.

This corporation has played an active role in marketing agricultural produce in the state. Between 1994-95 and 1998-99, it was engaged in the purchase and sale of chilli and ginger in the state. This was done through appointed agencies like Cooperation Department and Association of Mizoram Economic Forum, Tribal Cooperative Marketing Development Federation of India Limited (TRIFED), and Mizoram Widow Association who purchased the local produce from the farmers at rates fixed by MAMCO Ltd. From 1999-2000, it started to purchase ginger, chilli, turmeric, and cotton at specified rates from the farmers through appointed contractors. These contractors were expected to sell the same to other parts of the country for domestic consumption or exports. This system lasted till 2007-08. A free sale policy which was found to be less ineffective than the former was then adopted from the harvesting season of 2008-09. This policy, till date, exists side by side with its direct purchase policy.

(c) Mizoram Food and Allied Industries Corporation Limited (MIFCO)

Like MAMCO Ltd, the thrust area of Mizoram Food and Allied Industries Corporation (MIFCO) Ltd is rapid development and promotion of food processing industries in Mizoram, rather than marketing of the unprocessed products in and outside the state. It was established as a state government undertaking on 19th December, 1989 with authorised share capital of Rs. 20 crores. The state's Industries Department is the nodal agency for this corporation. The main objectives of MIFCO Ltd are as follows:

1. To engage in the processing and preservation of food, milk, fish, fruits, vegetables, and all food items of animal, poultry, agricultural, or piscicultural origin.
2. To deal in processed food, plant/machinery, implements, accessories, and pre-requisites of food processing.
3. To render necessary assistance for processing and preservation of agricultural produce, forest produce, and produce of animal origin for the purposes of increasing quantity of availability or otherwise of subsidiary foods in all their forms and variations, either for export or consumption in the country.

MIFCO Ltd has played a significant role in the marketing of locally produced fruit items like passion fruit and pineapple. These fruit items are processed in the processing plants operated by this corporation and are sold in the retail outlets at different parts of the state. Presently, it has three food processing plants: (1) Fruit Juice Concentrate Plant and Food Park at Chhingchhip, Serchhip district; (2) Pork and Poultry Processing Plant at Zemabawk, Aizawl district; and (3) Food Processing Plant at Sairang, Aizawl district.

Cooperative Sector

Cooperative movement also has substantial contribution in the promotion of agricultural produce marketing in Mizoram. The first cooperative society, 'The Aizawl Trading Cooperative Society Ltd', was established in 1949 and the first Sub-Divisional Office was established in 1951 which was upgraded to District Office in 1956. After attaining statehood in 1986, the Cooperative Department was established and there are at present 1400 Cooperative Societies including 11 State Level Cooperative Societies, in various categories. The activities taken up by these cooperative societies differ according to their nature of formation and their objectives. While some societies are formed by a group of producers, some are established for marketing of agricultural products.

While dealing with marketing institutions in the state, one cannot overlook the significant contribution of various cooperative societies in promoting agriculture marketing in the state. To help in understanding the contribution of these societies, a brief outline of the cooperative marketing societies and their role in marketing is given below.

First, the state level cooperative societies which are directly or indirectly involved in agriculture production and marketing in the state are Mizoram State Cooperative Marketing and Consumer Federation Ltd. (MIZOFED) established in 1981, Mizoram Multi-Commodity ProducerCooperative Union Ltd. (MULCO) established in 1984, Mizoram State Agriculture, Horticulture and Marketing Cooperative Federation Ltd. (MAHFED) established in 1987, Mizoram Pig Producers Cooperative Federation Ltd. (PIGFED) established in 1989, Mizoram Cooperative Fish Farming Marketing and Processing Federation Ltd. (ZOFISFED) established in 1998 and Mizoram Sericulture Farming Cooperative Society Ltd. (MASCOS) established in 1999.

MIZOFED was initially created for marketing of agricultural goods and procurement of certain cash crops, minor products, etc. from small farmers and individuals. However, due to one cause or the other, it failed to make substantial headway and often incurred financial losses. At present, this institution has no interest in marketing farm produce and had completely switched over to the dealership of POL, LPG, and other manufactured goods. On the other hand, the main role played by MULCO is the procurement, processing and distribution of milk products in Mizoram. Presently, there are 34 societies registered under MULCO in the state. Meanwhile, the main activities of the remaining cooperatives societies are indicated by the name of the society (i.e. fish production for ZOFISFED, pig for PIGFED, and so on).

Second, there are 1389 primary cooperative societies of which many are involved in the marketing of agriculture produce directly or indirectly. Table 2.4 shows that almost half of the primary societies are engaged in agriculture and allied and livestock activities. So, the cooperative institutions with its different form from primary levels to the apex levels occupy an important place in the cultivation and marketing of agriculture produce in the state.

Table 2.4: Activity Wise Distribution of Primary Cooperative Societies in Mizoram

Sl. No.	*Nature*	*No. of Societies*	*Sl. No.*	*Nature*	*No. of Societies*
1.	Handloom	187	12.	Multipurpose	194
2.	Piggery	187	13.	Fishery	75
3.	Service	48	14.	Milk Producers	13
4.	Housing	7	15.	LAMPS	8
5.	Dairy	24	16.	Canteen	14
6.	Sericulture	38	17.	Oil Seed Growers	2
7.	Processing	1	18.	Livestock	41
8.	Consumer	124	19.	Multi-Commodity	53
9.	Farming	247	20.	Fruits and Vegetable	24
10.	Industrial	69	21.	Labour	7
11.	Poultry	20	22.	Marketing	6

Source: Cooperation Department, Government of Mizoram, 2012.

Private Institutions

It is of general acceptance that the private sector is the real driver of growth and development of a country because the scope of government intervention in the working of the economy is limited by a number of constraints. This is also true for marketing of agricultural produce because the major portion of the commodity flow in the market is constituted by private stakeholders. However, it is hard to find private marketing stakeholders working on an organised basis in most of the underdeveloped countries. In Mizoram, various stakeholders like middlemen, wholesalers, retailers, etc. sell commodities in whatever way they can so as to ensure maximum profit. Such unorganised nature of private marketing institution, most of the time results in loss for the producers. Though there are a number of such organisations in the state, only some of the existing private institutions are discussed here. In addition to these, NGOs dealing in the marketing of agricultural produce in the state are also included.

Some of the state level NGOs and private institutions directly or indirectly operating in the field of agriculture marketing are — Hnamchhantu Pawl (HCP), Zopar Export Private Limited (ZEP), All Mizoram Farmers Union (AMFU), Community Development Action and Reflection (CDAR), and Mizoram Cultivator and Labour Union (MICLUN). A registered body under Firms and Society Registration Act, HCP is involved in the purchase, processing, and marketing of brooms in Mizoram, and is the most prominent marketing channel of broom in the state. Second, the main activity of ZEP, an incorporated body registered under Companies Registration Act, is marketing anthurium flowers from the state to domestic and export markets. Third, AMFU and MICLUN are farmers' organisations that work for the development and improvement of farming practice, production, and marketing of agriculture in the state. Fourth, CDAR was set up in the year 2007 for the upliftment of the poor and marginalised sections of the society. This organisation works for the processing and marketing of ginger and chilli in the state.

At the same time, traders (floating traders) from other Indian states occupy a crucial part in the marketing of agricultural products. They are called *Marwari,* the name of one Indian ethnic group of Rajasthan origin who are known for their business skills and trading success in the country. These people frequent the state, even the interior areas, throughout the year to procure surplus production of cash crops and transport the commodity they had purchased from the farmers to their base, generally located in Cachar District of Assam. The commodities generally procured from the state are ginger, chilli, areca-nut, orange, squash, turmeric, banana, and broom. It had been experienced that the time of harvest for some of the cash crops of Mizoram influences the time of arrival of the *Marwaris* in the local villages. Moreover, they are also the main agents for the import of vegetables like potato, fish, cabbage, cauliflower, onion, garlic, etc. from other states. Therefore, these agents play a significant role in the flow of agricultural products to and from the state.

Associations

A typical feature of marketing in the state is the presence of and role played by various associations. Businessmen or farmers dealing in the same commodities in certain areas usually form themselves in associations in order to protect their welfare. So, there is a complicated network of associations of different sorts in the state that are very influential in their respective areas in terms of price controls and prevention of the entry from outside. These associations take different forms at various levels village, block, district, state, specific area (markets). In respect to agriculture produce marketing, these associations may be broadly classified into 3 major groups as farmers/producers/growers/association, wholesalers/commission agents association, and retailers associations.

First, growers or farmers organise themselves in associations at different levels of state, district, and the like. Some examples are Mizoram Iskut (Squash) Growers Association (MIGA), Broom Cultivators Association of Mizoram (BCAM), Rubber Planters Association (RPA), Ginger Growers Associations in various villages, Arecanut Growers Association, Hmeithai (Widowed) Association, etc. These associations provide logistic for cultivation and the marketing of their products to the producers. They try and protect their members from unwanted situations like exploitation by traders and marketing intermediaries. For example, MIGA acts as the main institution for marketing squash in

Mizoram. Similarly, ginger growers association in various villages take up active steps to ensure remunerative procurement prices of ginger in their respective village areas.

Second, there are associations of middlemen/wholesale commission agents. A good example of such association would be Mahni Thlai Zuar Association (MTZA). Members of this association purchase vegetables and fruits from the producers in different parts of the state and sell them to the retailers in the nearby market stations, generally Aizawl and other district capitals. As far as possible, the MTZA fix the minimum procurement and wholesale prices which the members have to follow while dealing with such commodities in order to avoid price competition among themselves. However, depending on the venue and means of available communication, this association allows variation in the procurement prices sometimes. The role of middlemen/ wholesalers could also be seen from the experience of Mizo Panhnah Zuar Association (MPZA, Mizo Betel Leaf Sellers Association). In an attempt to protect themselves from price competition that may arise on account of non-local dealers of the same commodity, they put a ban on the import of betel leaf by outside traders, except theirs. As a result, non-local traders of this commodity put blockade of the same in Cachar district of Assam, the main route of imports to Mizoram. As a result of this misunderstanding, supply of the commodity reduced significantly for few weeks.

Third, retailer associations occupy a very important place in the marketing of agricultural products in the state. It was found during the field work that there are associations of vegetable sellers in each market, like the Vegetable Sellers Association, New Market, Aizawl; Bazaar Thu Association (Bazaar vendors Association); etc. The main objective of these associations is to protect the welfare of their members, especially on account of losses resulting from price competition. They impose regulations on retail prices in their respective market areas. Though they usually fix prices for the different commodities, they also allow heavy price reduction to enable these vendors distress sale in order to avoid spoilage of the commodities. This is mainly due to insufficiency of storage facility accessible by these petty vendors.

Conclusion

Notwithstanding the relevance of agriculture market regulation and the efforts of the government to put in place a well-regulated system to protect the interest of the farmers by enforcing several laws and rules, a regulated market is hard to come by in the context of Mizoram till today. Agriculture marketing in most of the cases is still at the hands of an unorganised network of middlemen, commission agents, traders, etc. with no efficient mechanism for timely disposal of market information. Further, infrastructural deficiency is another lacuna on agricultural marketing in Mizoram. The apparent symptom of such situations is the weak bargaining strength of the farmers/producers in the disposal of their produce, which usually end in unremunerative prices.

Of the mentioned marketing institutions at work in the state, majority of the market volume in the state is in the hands of private institutions. At the same time, associations of different types also play an active part in the market. In fact, these associations can also be clubbed under the broad category of private institution. Thus, a network of middlemen, wholesalers, retailers, and other organised body in the private sector are the main actors in the agriculture market of the state. This clearly indicates the minimal role played by the state government and its institutions in the prevailing market scenario.

3

Marketing of Homegrown Produce Outside the State

The system of Jhum cultivation has been practised extensively in Mizoram since time immemorial; and crops cultivated were for their own consumption and not for sale. Paddy was the main crop with other crops like chilli, ginger, etc. being secondary for a very long time. However, with a decline in soil fertility and the resulting lower paddy production coupled with the onset of economic development, people began to realise the significance of cultivating cash crops. Selling of home-grown produce was thus started. The system of settled cultivation was also started by the introduction to cash crops, while crops grown in Jhum land did not cease but existed side by side. In their search for better market opportunities, the people have managed to cross the state boundary. Today, there are many agricultural commodities marketed outside the state through various suitable channels.

This chapter focuses on the existing framework of marketing channels and institutions for five selected commodities ginger, squash, areca-nut, broom, and anthurium flower exported from the state. Even though certain amounts of these items are marketed in the local market, outside markets play a significant role.

Ginger

Ginger is one of the most important cash crops in Mizoram. It is generally grown in Jhum land. As the agro-climatic conditions of the state is favourable for its cultivation, ginger has been grown since long time back for own consumption as one of the secondary crops, without the use of manures, fertilisers or pesticides. Its cultivation as a cash crop in the state is known to have started in late 70s. There are three major varieties of ginger grown in the state namely *Thingpui, Thinglaidum,* and *Thingria* of which *Thinglaidum* is the most popular. A local variety called *Nadia,* which has low fibre content, was also introduced by Agriculture Department of Mizoram in the early 80s and is still grown in some areas, but only in small quantities. However, what has been experienced is that the variety of ginger does not seem to have any implication in the market price and avenues; and hence, most of the local farmers are unaware of the variety they grow. In fact, the marketing actors (traders) themselves are also unaware of varietal difference and its implication for further market. There seems to be no polarity in demand based on the variety of ginger as the actors are ready to purchase any type of ginger at the prevailing prices.

Mizoram had produced large amount of ginger during the last ten years. As per the record of the Directorate of Economics and Statistics, New Delhi (2010), Mizoram ranks fifth (5th) in terms of area and production of ginger in the country with a share of 7.8 per cent of the country's total production. The official record of area under cultivation and production of ginger in Mizoram during 2001-02 to 2010-11 is given in Table 3.1.

Market Channels

Availabilities of market avenues and price conditions generally determine the harvesting time of ginger in the state which normally

Table 3.1: Area and Production of Ginger in Mizoram

Year	*Area (In Hectare)*	*Production (in Metric Tonnes)*
2001-02	7287	46648
2002-03	5097	31136
2003-04	4481	29582
2004-05	4532	38068
2005-06	4654	45143
2006-07	3426	55432
2007-08	3587	57010
2008-09	10391	34290
2009-10	6200	31000
2010-11	6500	32500

Source: Horticulture Department, Govt. of Mizoram, 2013.

starts from November till May with January-April being the peak period. Market signals are perceived by the farmers when some traders from neighbouring states come to their village in search of ginger. The farmers do not make any arrangement in respect of grading and sorting by variety or size. The produce is simply packed in gunny bags whatever the status may be - whether clean or unclean, broken or whole, and the same is transported to the nearest roadside where it is piled up to wait for prospective buyers.

It is surprising to note that there is no organised market channel for ginger which is supposed to be in place since the crop is the most important cash crop (one dare say) and had been a political ball for many years. Its market remains uncertain and is characterised by chance factors. The system of ginger marketing is, thus, very complicated and difficult to present in clear cut patterns. Normally, petty traders and agents (both local and outside) of trading establishments located in the neighbouring state of Assam come to the village to collect the commodity. These marketing agents would, in turn, transport the same to the wholesale traders operating in Assam, like Karimganj, Bagha, and Silchar for further dispatch to terminal market via Siliguri toKolkata, Azhadpur (Delhi), Amritsar, Mumbai etc. and through Karimganj to Bangladesh. The petty traders and agents would quote any rate and haggle with the ignorant farmers who are unaware of how its marketing is being operated outside the state.

As per the information obtained from the farmers contacted from the 6 sampled villages, a summary of the existing marketing channels for ginger can broadly be identified. This is presented in Table 3.2. Of the three main marketing channels, Channel II and III assumes major importance because the local consumption, which is identified in Channel I, occupies a relatively small amount and is quite negligible.

Table 3.2: Marketing Channel of Ginger

Channel I	Producer—Retailer (Local market)—Consumer
Channel II	Producer—Local Trader— Wholesaler/Traders (Cachar/Silliguri)—Exporter in Terminal market (Bangladesh and Calcutta and Azhadpur (Delhi))—Consumer
Channel III	Producer—Local (Commission) agent—Itinerants dealers (Local and Outside)—Wholesaler/Traders (Cachar/Silliguri)—Exporter in Terminal market (Bangladesh and Calcutta and Azhadpur-Delhi)—Consumer

First, in Channel II, local traders collect the commodities by putting in place various collection points along the roadside of the villages. They normally purchase the produce at a price which is lower than the prevailing wholesale prices (around Re. 0.50) of the next destination. Once they have collected enough quantities, they move the same in bulk to the main collection areas located in Assam and West Bengal, usually Bagha, Silchar, and Siliguri, by making their own transport arrangement. They sell the produce in bulk to the wholesale dealers in these areas and earn certain amounts of profit. These actors or local traders serve as an important link between producers and wholesalers at the selling point. However, it is difficult to trace the movement of these commodities once it passes through the main collection points of Assam. As per the available information, after reaching the main market terminal in some major cities, the commodity is processed (grading, packaging, cleaning, etc.) and then passed on for sale in either the local or export markets.

Second, in Channel III, the main actor at the village level appears to be *Local (Commission) Agent* and the *Itinerant Traders* who hail from both local and other states. The commission agents in the village collect the commodity at the prices authorised by the itinerant traders and he/she would be given a certain fraction of the price as dealing charge. The Itinerant Traders, on their part, provided the local agents with funds and gunny bags, respectively for collection/procurement and packing the ginger. The same would, then, be transported by the *itinerant* traders to the wholesalers trading in the next destination, like Bagha market of Cachar areas and Siliguri. The wholesalers further move the commodity to dealers located in other parts of the country.

Information obtained from the 6 selected villages as presented in Table 3.3 reveals that more than 69 per cent of the farmers and more than 70 per cent of the products are directly sold to the *Local Commission Agent*. At the same time, selling to the local trader (who is also a producer) constituted 28.65 per cent of the total output.

Seasonal Variations of Arrivals and Prices

In a competitive marketing system, arrival determines the prices of farm commodities. However, the ginger market in Mizoram does not show any systematic causal effect of market arrivals on

Table 3.3: Marketing Agents of Ginger in the Sampled Villages

Channel	Marketing Agent/Institutions	No. of Households/Farmers	Amount (In qts.)
I	Retailer (Local Market)	4 (1.33)	325 (0.90)
II	Local trader cum producer	89 (29.57)	10352.7 (28.65)
III	Local (Commission) Agent	208 (69.10)	25456.2 (70.45)
	Total	301 (100.00)	36133.9 (100.00)

* Figure in Parentheses show Percentage

Source: Sample survey, 2013.

its prices; but rather, the price level has been shown as the main determinant of market arrivals. This situation may be taken as an imperfect market with unresponsive price to arrivals, which may end in perpetual distress for the farmers. Moreover, as ginger grown in a current year can be kept for harvest in the next year, farmers often prefer not to harvest the produce if they find the prevailing price to be unprofitable. At the same time, some farmers prefer to wait for favourable prices which usually take place at the start of monsoon season (i.e. May – June). Accordingly, the marketing season usually starts in the month of November and ends in June; and the off season starts from July and last till October.

To show this aspect of ginger marketing in Mizoram, the trends showing the market arrivals and prices, as recalled by some knowledgeable persons in the selected villages, are presented in Table 3.4.

Public Intervention on Ginger Market

With ginger being extensively cultivated in most of the villages for the last many years, public intervention on the matter is crucial to protect the poor farmers from market risk resulting from open competition. To this effect, the Government of Mizoram in the past years had played a key role in procuring ginger produce directly or by appointing registered buyers (contractors). During the 1996-97 and 1997-98 marketing season, a government agency called the Mizoram Agricultural Marketing Corporation Limited (MAMCO)

Table 3.4: Trends in the Arrival and Prices of Ginger in the Selected Villages

Months	2010-11		2011-12		2012-13	
	Arrival	Price/Qtls	Arrival	Price/Qtls	Arrrival	Price/ Qtls
November	701.8 (5.24)	500	307 (4.66)	300	773 (5.10)	1100
December	1423.7 (10.64)	650	986.5 (14.98)	350	1513.4 (9.99)	1500
January	3515 (26.26)	700	2228.5 (33.84)	500	3916 (25.85)	1700
February	4500.3 (33.62)	1150	1327.7 (20.16)	400	5132.1 (33.88)	1850
March	1784.4 (13.33)	1400	706 (10.72)	500	2347.5 (15.50)	3000
April	815 (6.09)	1600	390 (5.92)	550	1023 (6.75)	3400
May	370 (2.76)	1950	406 (6.17)	700	308 (2.03)	3800
June	274 (2.05)	2400	233 (3.54)	700	136.5 (.90)	5000
Total	13384.2 (100.00)		6584.7 (100.00)		15149.5 (100.00)	

Source: Sample survey, 2013

* Sample Village – Mualpheng, Ruallung, Rulchawm, Sateek, Tachhip and Thiak

* Figure in Parenthesis Show Percentage of Arrivals

was entrusted to purchase ginger directly from the producers for possible resale to other traders/exporters. However, due to one cause or the other, the entire procurement plan and the marketing strategy failed, which resulted in huge financial loss to the government to the tune of Rs. 4 crores. As a result, MAMCO discontinued the policy of purchasing ginger directly from the farmers.

Towards the start of marketing season in 1998-99, the state government again instituted indirect market intervention policy by appointing 12 registered/monopolistic buyers for 7 collection centres identified by MAMCO Ltd. Under this system, nobody, including the farmers themselves, were allowed to sell ginger to any other traders, except by government appointed contractors. The appointed contractors were expected to abide by the marketing policy set out by the government with respect to floor rate, which was revised from time to time to suit outside market environment. However, due to lack of professional skills among the contractors, they were unable to sell the quantitiesthey had purchased from the farmers to bigger market terminals located in major cities like Delhi, Calcutta, Siliguri, etc. for sale within the country and possible export. They, reportedly, sold them to the wholesale dealers operating in the nearby Cachar district of Assam. As these contractors had strong influence on the price of ginger in the state, unfavorable sticky price haunted ginger growers of the state for many years. Again, the government policy had failed.

Due to constant pressure from farmers and several marketing experts, the state government decided to roll back its agricultural marketing policy with effect from the marketing season of 2008-09 giving birth to a more or less new strategy. This new strategy emphasised on "Free Sale Policy" by repealing the earlier rules which allowed any person or agency to purchase and transport ginger in and outside the state by issuing permits through MAMCO Ltd. Since then, the role of government in ginger marketing was reduced to a mere facilitator, rather than regulator. According to the producers interviewed during the field work, the price of ginger responded positively to the new policy and has increased year after year which undoubtedly is an advantage for the farmers.

Squash (Chayote)

The cultivation of squash in Mizoram is known to have started with the coming of western Christian missionaries. Squash being a minor cucurbit was not cultivated extensively and was not a commercialised vegetable in other parts of the country at the time of its introduction in Mizoram. Its cultivation in large scale was taken up only in Mizoram during those days. As a semi-perennial crop, it requires moderate climate with good humidity as prevalent in Bangalore, lower hills of Darjeeling, North East India, and Koraput region of Orissa. Therefore, the state was found ideal for its successful cultivation considering its soil and climatic conditions. The fruits, tender leaves, and root tubers of a squash plant can be consumed.

There are different varieties of squash classified according to its shape and colour, i.e. *Round white, Long white, Pointed green, Broad green,* and *Oval green*. Normally, two types of greenand other creamy green are grown in Bangalore and North Eastern region. A well-grown plant of about one year old yields 500-600 fruits per year and weights 200-450 grams each; and lasts for 3-4 years.

Large scale cultivation of squash was done only since the 1980s when farmers of Sihphir village initiated its cultivation for onward adoption to their permanent livelihood, and as an alternative to unsustainable practice of Jhumming. As of now, there are around 1200-1600 families engaged in its cultivation. These farmers are spread in the villages in and around Sihphir within Aizawl and Kolasib districts, viz. Sihphir Vengthar, Sihphir Neihbawih, Lungdai, Serkhan, Nisapui, and in other villages although at a smaller scale. Unfavourable climatic condition in the neighbouring state of Assam has made its cultivation more attractive with potential marketing opportunities in Cachar district of Assam, like Karimganj, Silchar, Bagha, and Hailakandi. Thus, it is one of the most important crops grown and exported from Mizoram in huge quantities. To facilitate its marketing, a well-organized society, named "Mizoram Iskut Growers' Association" (MIGA) was formed in 1982 with its headquarters at Sihphir village.

The increase in area under squash cultivation and production in Mizoram during 2003-2013 is presented in Table 3.5. The implementation of Technology Mission in the state during 2008-09 also had great impact on its production and area expansion.

Table 3.5: Area and Production of Squash in Mizoram 2003-2013

Year	*Area (in Hectare)*	*Production (in Metric Ton)*
2003-04	580	20949
2004-05	583	19886
2005-06	604	21593
2006-07	664	24455
2007-08	714	26418
2008-09	3200	48000
2009-10	2250	34875
2010-11	3500	56350
2011-12	4000	66500
2012-13	4250	73525

Source: Dept. of Horticulture, Government of Mizoram, 2013.

Marketing Practices

Squash cultivation is characterised by a relatively well-organised marketing channel, when compared with other cash crops grown in the state. Harvesting season starts at the onset of monsoon during April-May when its price starts to rise; and its price drops during its peak season, August-September. This crop shows a long harvesting period lasting up to January of the next year. However, due to the absence of proper storage facilities, farmers do not have retaining power to take full advantage of temporal variations in price. They have to sell the commodities right after it is harvested to whatever channel is available at that time. A notable feature of its marketing is the role played by 'Mizoram Iskut Growers' Association' (MIGA) which functions as an institution to counter-balance the possible price competition arising out of monopolistic control by traders or trading establishment and other marketing establishments. A thorough examination of the existing market flow shows that there are three main marketing channels for this crop. They are given in Table 3.6.

Table 3.6: Major Marketing Channels of Squash

Channel I	Producer—Wholesale Commission Agent (Local)—Retailer (Local market)—Consumer
Channel II	Producer—Local Trader—Wholesaler/Traders (Cachar Areas)—Retailer (Cachar areas)—Consumer
Channel III	Producer—Local (Commission) agent—Itinerants dealers (Local and Outside)— Wholesaler/ Traders (Cachar Areas)—Retailer (Cacher areas)—Consumer

First, due to increasing consumption within the state, Channel I occupies a prominent place in the marketing of squash. The main actors in this channel are wholesale commission agent who have direct contact with the producers and transport the commodities to retailers operating in different market places of the state. They organise themselves in an association, named 'Mahni Thlai Zuar Association (MZTA)' (Own Produce Vegetable Marketing Association), and actually function as wholesalers, in addition to marketing of their produce. Depending on the prevailing producer's price, MZTA has strong influence on the wholesale price of squash. Though attempt was made to assess the price margins or value chain in order to estimate producers' share in the final price, it was not successful as these marketing agents were unable to furnish the required information.

Second, *local traders* play an important role in Channel II. They collect the commodities in and around their villages and carried the same in bulk to the wholesale dealers operating in market terminals of Assam and earn a certain amount of profit in the process. Third, it was observed that some middlemen are facilitating local men with fund and material for the collection of the commodity and are offered certain margin as dealing charge. The facilitator traders are called *itinerant dealers* and the ones they facilitated are the *local commission agent.* The immediate destination of all these agents remains to be Karimganj, Bagha, Hailakandi, and Silchar in Assam state till date.

It may also be noted here that Mizoram has exported huge amount of squash to Assam state since long time back. The official record showing the trend of squash export to Assam since 1999 is presented in Table 3.7. Unfortunately, it is very difficult to assess the wholesale or retail prices in these market destinations and hence, it is not possible to estimate the value chain for this commodity.

Table 3.7: Export of Squash Outside the State from 1999-2000

Sl. No.	*Year*	*Amount (In Qtls)*
1.	1999-00	60000
2.	2000-01	88735
3.	2003-04	16405
4.	2004-05	63116
5.	2005-06	9609
6.	2006-07	75512
7.	2007-08	28044
8.	2008-09	28431
9.	2009-10	21189
10.	2010-11	87449
11.	2011-12	38920

Source: Trade and Commerce Dept., Govt. of Mizoram, 2013.

An interview of 48 selected squash farmers in Sihphir village during the field work revealed that more than 53 per cent (Table 3.8) of the total produce during 2012-13 was sold through *local commission agents* (as in Channel III above). At the same time,

Table 3.8: Agents of Squash Market in Mizoram

Channel	Agents/Institutions	No of farmers	Amount (In qts)
I	Wholesale Commission Agent (Local)	6 (12.5)	8616.68 (11.59)
II	Local trader	18 (37.5)	25920.92 (34.85)
III	Local (Commission) Agent	24 (50.00)	39839.32 (53.56)
	Total	48 (100.00)	74376.92 (100.00)

* Figure in Parentheses show Percentage

Source: Sample Survey, 2013.

marketing through local traders also contributed a significant portion (34.85 percent), while 11.59 per cent of the total produce was sold in the local market (within the State) through local wholesale commission agents.

Role of Mizoram Iskut (Squash) Growers' Association (MIGA)

To organise and facilitate squash growers in the State, the Mizoram Iskut Growers' Association (MIGA) was formed in 1982 with its headquarters at Sihphir village. At present, the Association has branches in 9 villages with a total membership of more than 500 farmers. MIGA has its branches in the villages mainly where there are enough surplus production of squash - they are *N. Chaltlang, Lungmuat, Serkhan, Nisapui, North Bualpui, Lungdai, Sihphir Neihbawih, Sihphir,* and *Sihphir Vengthar.* The main objective of this association is to initiate a better and a more efficient marketing system vis-a-vis cultivation of squash to its members. To achieve this objective, it had instituted several strategies since the mid-80s.

First, *'Quota System'* was introduced to check flooding of market and its subsequent price crash. Under this raj, the state's Trade and Commerce Department, in consultation with the Association, gave permit/license and appointed marketing contractors to buy the commodity from the growers. This Association, on its part, decided to form groups consisting of few growers and each group was allocated a day or two to sell their produce on rotational basis. The size of the group was determined according to the volume of their produce to prevent flooding of market and the potential price crash in the market destination (normally Cachar District of Assam). *Quota System* was also facilitated by the government by providing price support subsidy for some time. This system of squash marketing ran smoothly for some time with a price-support subsidy extended to the growers by the government during 1994-95 and 1995-96 (*Lianzela, 1996*). In addition to price subsidy, the government offered minimum procurement price to the extent of Rs. 1.25 per kilogram to the farmers since the marketing season of 1996-97. However, the new Market Intervention Scheme of the government did not get much response from the growers and was consequently discontinued.

Second, with the increase in production, withdrawal of price support subsidy from the government, and the coming of new entrants in squash market (i.e. Meghalaya) in the late 90s, *Quota System* did not work well to the satisfaction of farmers. MIGA in its search for new marketing avenues conducted a market survey under financial support of North Eastern Council (NEC) which covered markets in New Delhi, Sikkim, Shimla, and some other cities. Based on this market study, MIGA finally decided to do away the *'quota system'* and instituted *'free marketing system'* since 2000 till date. Under the new system, every producer was given liberty to sell his/her produce any time and place, whenever and wherever he/she thinks is profitable.

Quantity Arrival and Price

To have a clear picture on the seasonal conditions of squash marketing in terms of marketing seasons and price trends, the monthly quantity arrival and price data was collected from Sihphir village as recorded by MIGA. This is presented in Table 3.9. The trend shown by the two economic variables, price and quantity arrival, somehow, is in consonance with the traditional demand theory, in contrast to ginger. One may conclude that there is efficiency in squash market at least to some extent.

Areca-Nut

Areca-nut is grown in the western and north western lowland. Its plantation was started in the state by some villages around the

Table 3.9: Monthly Quantity Arrivals and Price of Squash in Sihphir Market

Month	*2011-12*		*2011-12*		*2012-13*	
	Arrival (Qtl.)	*Price (Rs./Qtl.)*	*Arrival (Qtl.)*	*Price (Rs./Qtl.)*	*Arrival (Qtl.)*	*Price (Rs./Qtl.)*
April	250.6	2200	248.7	2150	231.95	3000
May	723.7	1500	639.45	1100	717.6	1900
June	1456	800	1483.04	750	1482.8	750
July	4788.7	700	4813.52	600	5043.99	650
August	8125.9	500	8333.12	400	8588	600
September	9124.8	300	8874.04	250	9577.35	275
October	6007	375	5754.37	350	6471.1	320
November	3323.8	400	3356.44	400	3392.49	400
December	1867.3	500	1923	450	1865.96	450
January	1256.3	550	843	500	737	500
Total	36924.1		36268.68		38108.24	

Source: Sample survey 2013.

Assam state boundary during the 1970s and was later extended to other low lying areas. It has recorded a significant expansion in terms of area and production in the state, especially after the implementation of New Land Use Policy (NLUP) by the state government in 1993-94 and 2010-11. As per the official records, the total production stood at 12,390 Metric Tonnes with cultivated area of 5,010 hectares during 2011-12. The growth in areca-nut production and area expansion in the state is presented in Table 3.10.

Table 3.10: Growth of Area under Areca-nut Cultivation and Production in Mizoram

Year	*Area (in Hectare)*	*Production (in Metric Tonnes)*
2001-02	1334	1057
2002-03	1709	5736
2004-05	1341	5095
2005-06	1378	4134
2010-11	4800	12200
2011-12	5010	12390

Source: Various issues of 'Statistical Handbook of Mizoram', Directorate of Economics and Statistics, Government of Mizoram.

Areca-nut is extensively cultivated in western and north western parts of the state within Kolasib and Mamit districts. To represent these two districts, two villages, Zamuang and Bilkhawthlir in Mamit and Kolasib districts, respectively, were selected for this study. The two selected villages are known for their success in the cultivation of areca-nut and the existing marketing practices in these villages are expected to represent areca-nut marketing in the state.

Market Channels

It was observed that there is an unorganised but systematic flow of areca-nut market in the two areas. Neither the producers nor its facilitator NGO, like 'Kuhva Ching Association' (Arecanut Growers Association), have clear information regarding the price trends and quantity arrivals. All that can be assessed from the sample producers is a rough estimate. This is because majority of the produce is sold in grove while the nuts are still tender. The buyers are normally commission agents from the state of Assam who purchase the areca-nut groves at least two months before the actual harvesting time. Harvesting and transportation are in the hands of these commission agents. Actually, the producer takes up just the responsibility of clearing the plantation field. It is, therefore, not an easy task to collect information on the output and producer's price. Based on the information obtained from an interview of knowledgeable persons and leaders of the growers associations, market channels presented in Figure 3.1 are identified for areca-nut in Mizoram.

First, *non-local commission agents,* normally from Assam, arrive at the village during *October – November* to purchase the areca-nut in groves while the nuts are tender. The price of areca-nut is quoted based on the expected number of nuts in each tree. Normally, they pay Rs. 110-120 per tree, which may be reduced to Rs. 100 depending on its accessibility. It was reported that one tree usually bears 200-400 nuts. After this process is completed, they would leave and then come back in the months of *January-February* for the harvest. They carry the same in bulk to the *wholesalers*operating in the neighbouring state of Assam. These wholesalers keep the commodity in storage centres (called *Skops*), operated either by themselves or others, for resale as and when there is demand from

Figure 3.1: Flow Chart of the Major Marketing Channels for Arecanut in Mizoram

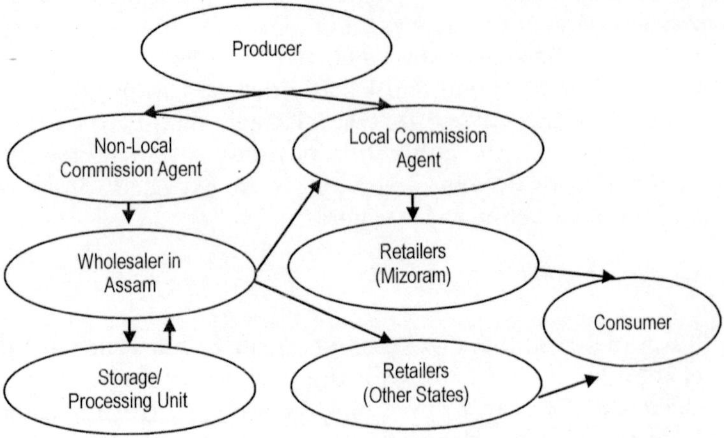

Table 3.11: Marketing Channels of Areca-nut in Mizoram

Channel I	Producer— Non-Local Commission Agent—Wholesaler (Assam) – Local Commission Agents – Retailers – Consumers
Channel II	Producer— Non-Local Commission Agent—Wholesaler (Assam) – Retailers (other States)– Consumers
Channel III	Producer— Local Commission Agent—Retailers – Consumers

Mizoram and other states of India. As per the information obtained from the interview of areca-nut retailers in Aizawl market areas, *local commission agents* collect the commodity from these wholesale dealers at the prevailing wholesale prices and transport the same to Mizoram for onward delivery to retailers who then sell it to the consumers.

Second, Channel II follows the same pattern as Channel I except for the agents in the final stage of market chain. That is, the retailers mentioned in this channel are operating in other states. However, the process of how the commodities are obtained from the wholesalers operating in Assam cannot be ascertained. Third, the marketing channel of certain quantities of the produce which the producer reserves for sale in local market and own consumption is presented in Channel III. If it is meant for sale in bigger market destinations within the state, local commission agents would buy the commodities and sell the same to the retailers within the state. Generally, these quantities are marketed at relatively higher price during off-season, i.e. May-July.

In our attempt to evaluate the value chain for areca-nut from the two producing clusters, Zamuang and Bilkhawthlir, we estimated the average number of nuts borne by one areca-nut tree. Then we divide the average quoted price per tree of the commission agents by the estimated number of nuts per tree to arrive at the average producer's price per nut. Further, the average wholesale price charged by big wholesalers in the main market terminals (i.e. Assam) to the local commission agents, who would later on deliver the commodity to the retailers for sale in local market (Mizoram), was collected from the local commission agents. It should be noted that the results presented in this analysis are all rough estimates made on the basis of information obtained from interviewing some marketing stakeholders. In summary, the areca-nut produced in Mizoram is bought by outsiders from the state and local commission agents who again would bring back the same to Mizoram for resale.

The estimated value chain for this commodity is presented in Table 3.12. Though the table is but a rough estimate, it clearly indicates an interesting price chain for this commodity in the process of its entry into Assam and back to traders in Mizoram. The process goes like this: The non-local commission agents who

Table 3.12: Estimated Value Chain in the Marketing of Areca-nut in Mizoram

Rough Estimate

Surplus Production Centres	Producer Price (Re/No)	Wholesale Commission Price (Assam) (Rs./No)	Wholesale Commission Price from Wholesalers in Assam (Rs/No)	Selling Price by Local Commission Agent to Local Retailers (Rs/No)	Average Retailed Price in the final product (Rs./No)	Producer's Share in the Final Price (%)
Zamuang	0.4	0.75	1.5	2.76	4.5	8.9
Bilkhawthlir	0.25	0.5	1.15	2.41	3.9	6.4
Average	**0.32**	**0.62**	**1.32**	**2.58**	**4.2**	**7.6**

Source: Estimated from an Interview of Various Marketing Stakeholders during November 2013.

hail from Assam pay, on an average, 32 Paisa per nut at the farm gate and charges 62 Paisa to the big wholesaler dealers, who would store the commodity to wait for market demand. These wholesale dealers (cum storage agents) sell the commodity to the *local commission agent* by charging Rs. 1.32 per nut, and these agents would later deliver the same to the local retailers by charging Rs. 2.58 per nut. The retailers, in turn, after processing the commodities to its final form (*Kuhva*), can earn around Rs. 4.2 per nut with a profit margin of 63 per cent.

The estimated producer's share in the final price is extremely low in each of the cases. It is less than 10 per cent on an average. There may be a number of reasons for this pitiful state of areca-nut marketing in Mizoram. Some of them are (1) lack of well-organised marketing institution, (2) asymmetric information suffered by the producer towards the real stakeholders and price conditions in the subsequent market stages, and (3) lack of proper storage facilities which results in unnecessary transit of the commodity via Assam. Thus, an institution of a well-organised marketing chain with provisions of marketing infrastructure would be of much help to ensure that the producer earns maximum share in the final price and to reduce consumers' surplus loss.

Brooms

Broom grass is found and grown on damp steep banks, sandy banks of rivers, and on the slope of hills. The topography of Mizoram is thus favourable for the cultivation of broom grass. It, like other non-timber forest products, is more or less available throughout the year and can be grown even on marginal lands, wastelands, and Jhum fallow. Therefore, its cultivation can promote the sustainable use of fragile and degraded lands. The culms arise centrifugally during the peak growing season (usually April to July) and bear inflorescences which are about 30 to 90 cm long on shoot apex at the end of its vegetative growth. They are harvested on maturity during winter season. The harvested inflorescences are ultimately sold as broomsticks. Broom has emerged as one of the important produce because every household requires it. It enjoys substantial demand throughout the country and abroad. Moreover, as this commodity could be stored for a very long time, the producer can avail the benefits of temporal price variations and demand change.

In Mizoram, though broom grass is available throughout the state, they are relatively more abundant in the forest divisions of Kolasib, Kawrthah, and Darlawn. An interesting fact is that the price of broom grass is at most times higher in these forest divisions than in other divisions. The cultivation and harvesting of broom grass is controlled by the Divisional Forest Officer. There used to be a *mahaldari* system at work in the broom making avenue but was suspended in 2010 in hopes of attaining a more sustainable and profitable system of commercialising the state's forest resources. Moreover, in a step to protect the local farmers from exploitation, individuals from other states are denied harvesting permit. However, the local permit holders often sell their permits to other individuals mostly from other parts of the country. This has been reported to inhibit the local manufacturers in strive for a higher level of production and its subsequent profit.

Marketing Channels

There are two broad marketing channels in the state, viz. traditional marketing channel (like direct sale of the products, selling to commission agents, etc.) and emerging market channels (marketing through organised marketing institutions). Since the farmers themselves can make the final product for this commodity, i.e. broomstick, and can be stored by the farmers without any technical support, it can reach the consumer directly in its final form throughout the year. The main channels of its marketing as observed in the field work can be summarised in flow chart of Figure 3.2.

Marketing channels mentioned in the flow chart (Figure 3.2) are also given in Table 3.13. As mentioned above, these can be reclassified into traditional channel (Channel I and II) and emerging channel (Channel III and IV). The first two channels are in practice since long time; while the remaining two channels were instituted recently with the formation of facilitator agency in the state. While the emerging channel is running in an organised manner, the traditional channel does not. It should be noted that wild brooms also contribute a significant portion of market volume in the state. Accordingly, farmers who collect wild brooms from the forest are also considered as producers since they are in first contact with the commodity.

Figure 3.2: Flow Chart of Broom Marketing Channels in Mizoram

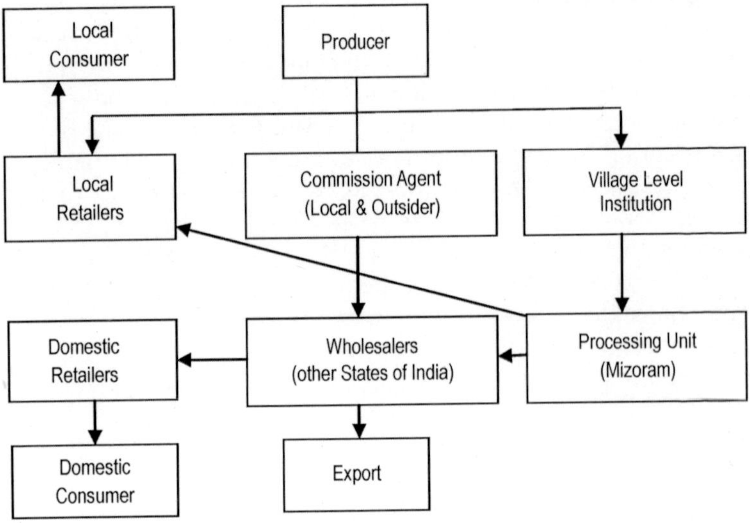

Table 3.13: Marketing Channels of Brooms in Mizoram

Channel - I	Producer—Retailer—Consumer
Channel - II	Producer—Middleman (Commission Agent) – Wholesaler — Domestic Retailer/Export – Consumer
Channel - III	Producer—Local Institution — Processing Unit (Workshop in the State Capital) — Wholesaler — Domestic Retailer/Export—Consumer
Channel - IV	Producer—Local Institution — Processing Unit (Workshop in the State Capital) — Retailer (local) – Consumer

As stated, since broom processing and making of broomstick and other products do not require much technical knowhow, the producers themselves can undertake it and sell them directly to the retailers or consumers. This case is presented in Channel I. As the producers have longer retaining capacity for raw brooms, this channel has been in place in the state for a long time. Second, in Channel II, there are some traders, *middlemen (commission agents),* who come to the village to collect broom (in its original form) from the producers. This channel is also prevalent in the state since long, probably when the people started marketing brooms. The agents transported the commodity beyond the state, normally to Assam, and sell it to the wholesalers for further processing who would later sell the same either to the domestic or export markets. These agents often get the support of local traders in the procurement and transportation of brooms from their respective villages.

Third, the main stakeholder in Channel III and IV is *Hnamchhantu Pawl (HCP)* and its network across the state. This organisation has its branches, or section, in different parts of the state and has opened 10 broom collection centres across the state. Their members brought the brooms they had collected from the farmers to these centres which would later be transported to its headquarters at Aizawl where it would be processed in its final form, i.e. broomsticks and other broom products. After completing the requirements of grading, weighting, binding/wrapping, and packaging at the general workshop of HCP at Aizawl, the products are sold to the agents of wholesalers from outside the state. Though certain amount is sold to the local retailers for local consumption, the major portion of the product is sold outside through these agents. It was reported that through this organization, the agents sell the commodity in big wholesale markets located in Delhi, Mumbai, Rajasthan, and Guwahati. According to the information obtained from the leaders of HCP, wholesalers dealing in Mumbai and Rajasthan exported the products to Iran and Afghanistan, in addition to their sale to local dealers; while the remaining centres are selling the products within the country.

Role of Hnamchhantu Pawl (HCP)

Hnamchhantu Pawl (HCP), an NGO, was formed on the 3rd March, 1994 by 6 members with R. Ramhmangaiha being the founder President. It was registered under Firms and Societies Registration Act, 1976 in the year 1995. This organisation has its headquarters in Electric Veng, Aizawl, and its main workshop at Republic Veng, Aizawl. Presently, it has more than 500 members across the state. The main objective of this organisation is to train the local unemployed youth for self-employment through broomstick making, fibre processing, cane and bamboo works, and other handicraft items. The product of these trained youths would be bought by the organisation, if they do not find market for their produce. It had also imparted training to more than 3000 local youths till date.

Before HCP entered the marketing of brooms, the entire broom market in the state was at the hands of few license holders (issued by the government) who outsourced the task to non-local commission agents. The system was found unprofitable for the producers as the prices were controlled by a network of few traders. To counteract the pricing monopoly power of these traders, HCP decided to step into the business of broom marketing in 1998 and has continued till date. Before, the existing market price was Rs. 3 per kg; but when the HCP bid the prevailing price by offering Rs. 6 per kg, the market price abruptly increased to Rs. 9 per kg. This clearly indicates the role of this organisation in protecting poor farmers from price fluctuations.

HCP has opened 10 broom collection centres throughout the state, where the farmers can sell their produce instead of transporting it to the headquarters for further processing. It charges a uniform price, i.e. Rs. 40 per kg (2013-14), in all these collection centres. As mentioned earlier, one of the main objectives of this organisation is to give training to unemployed youths for self-employment in making broomstick and other products of broom. These trained youths operate the collection centres and do the needful, like drying, cleaning, etc., before sending the produce to the headquarters in semi-processed forms. The commodity received in semi-processed form from these collection centres would further be processed by grading, weighing, packaging, and binding/wrapping with plastic in the main workshop of the organisation. Having done all these processes of value addition, the final products are collected by agents of wholesalers from outside the state like Delhi, Mumbai, Rajasthan, and Guwahati. It was stated that these agents are ready to come at any time when there is enough stock of broomsticks and other products. According to a reliable source, wholesalers dealing in Mumbai and Rajasthan are exporting the products they purchased from Mizoram to other countries like Iran, Afghanistan, etc.

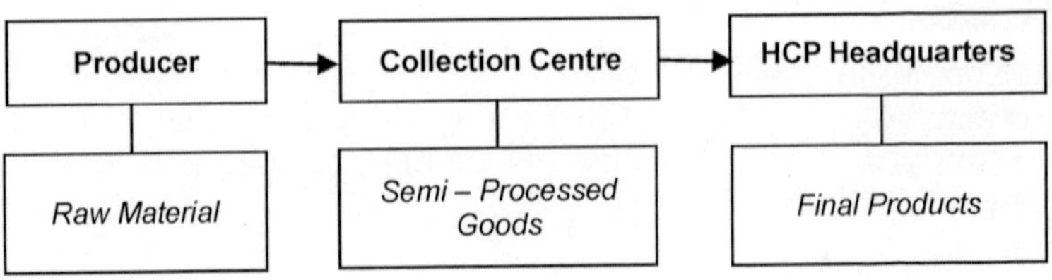

Public Intervention in Broom Market

Since broom is classified as a forest product, the state's Environment and Forest Department imposed royalty at the rate of Rs. 7 per kg till 2013. In fact, wild broom still contributes a large portion of brooms produced in the state. At the same time, the state government has adopted its cultivation as one of the activities under its flagship programme, New Land Use Policy (NLUP). As per the record of the Directorate of Economics and Statistics, Government of Mizoram, a large area of 3,872 hectares has been covered by broom cultivation under NLUP during 2011-12. Considering the state government's initiative to encourage broom cultivation as an alternative to Jhumming, it was felt that imposition of royalty could discourage to the farmers, and consequently, the state government decided to reduce the royalty from Rs. 7 to Rs. 3.50 per kilogram in the later part of 2013. At the same time, it gave tax holiday to any final product of broom. The same is also extended to broom produced by NLUP beneficiaries upon the fulfilment of certain requirements. Further, to facilitate better marketing channel and chain of value addition, the state government decided to give free interest loan to the tune of Rs. 150 lakhs to *Hnamchhantu Pawl* (HCP) from the NLUP scheme in 2013. During 2012-13, HCP collected 4250 quintals of raw broom from producers/farmers.

Value Chain of Brooms

Raw brooms are broadly classified into two classes, No. 1 and 2 according to its size and length. While No. 1 raw broom can fetch 3.3 broomsticks per kilogram on an average, No. 2 can fetch 2.3 per kg. Thus, a kilogram of unprocessed broom could be processed to 2-3 broomsticks. At the same time, while the prevailing procurement price ranged from Rs. 30 to Rs. 60 per kg in the open market, the price offered by *Hnamchhantu Pawl* is Rs. 40 per kg. Since we do not have the required information on the value chain of broom market in case of the former, only the value chain of broom through HCP is presented in Table 3.14.

An interesting feature of the value chain given in Table 3.14 is the producers' share in the final price (in its final products). It is on average 52.91 per cent which is very impressive, if we take into

Table 3.14: Value Chain of Broom Marketing in Mizoram through Hnamchhantu Pawl

Procure-ment Price (Rs/Kg)	*Class*	*Broom-stick per Kg (No)*	*Production Cost (Rs/Pcs)*	*Final Price (Rs/Pcs)*	*Estimated Amount per Kg (Rs) (Col.3 x5)*	*Producer's Share in the Final Price (%)*
1	2	3	4	5	6	7
40	No. 1	3.3	20.75	27	89.1	44.89
	No. 2	2.3	24	27	62.1	64.41
Average		**2.8**	**22.38**	**27**	**75.6**	**52.91**

Source: Hnamchhantu Pawl, January 2014.

account the producer share in case of areca-nut (less than 10 per cent). This is an indication of the advantage of a well-organised marketing channel, which enable impressive earnings to the producers without unreasonable increase in the prices of final products.

Anthurium Flower

Anthurium flowers are perennial herbaceous plant of great beauty and are grown for their showy cut flowers or for their attractive foliage. Since the mid-1980s, its popularity has increased dramatically and now has become a popular addition to foliage growers. The life span of the plant is 6-8 years. It enjoys popularity in domestic as well as export markets, and the locally produced flowers are sold at reasonable prices. Its export possibility appears quite promising as the flower has already been exported to the Middle East (Singh, 2006). Cultivation of anthurium was introduced for the first time in Mizoram by the state's Department of Horticulture in November 2002 under Technology Mission.

The ideal condition for its successful cultivation ranges between 15°C-32°C. Thus, the climatic condition of Mizoram is highly conducive for the cultivation of this flower as the temperature ranges between 18°C-30°C during summer and 8°C-24°C during winter. The anthurium flowers produced in the state are of high quality, so much so that it has earned a niche in being one of the commodities exported to other countries. Immediately after its introduction in the state, the cut flowers of anthurium are exported to other countries in October 2003 through a Bangalore based Export Company named Zopar Export Private Limited. The first shipment of 1000 anthurium cut flowers from Mizoram and Meghalaya was exported to Al Lokrit, Dubai which is one of the biggest wholesalers in West Asia. If we take into account the increasing demand of anthurium flower for domestic and international markets with ideal climatic conditions of Mizoram, its extensive cultivation has the potential to boost the state's economy. However, one cannot deny that well-organised marketing institutions and channels with basic infrastructure would be of crucial importance to facilitate the increasing production.

The state government initiated cultivation of this flower in 2002 under the Technology Mission scheme with Horticulture Department as its nodal department. It has been classified as one of the horticulture crops. In this initiative, the government imported quality planting materials from the Netherlands and supplied them to selected growers. These growers were also given shade nets and other inputs like coco pea, water tank, sprinkler irrigation, etc. Production of cut flowers and cultivation areas has increased tremendously since its introduction in the state. This is presented in Table 3.15.

Marketing Stakeholders

The existence of a well-organised, efficient, and responsive marketing institution is a precondition for the successful cultivation of any crop. Exposing anthurium growers who lack

Table 3.15: Area and Production of Anthurium in Mizoram: (2004-05 to 2010-11)

Year	*Area (Hectares)*	*Production (in lakh No)*
2004-05	4.22	0.19
2005-06	5.44	0.44
2006-07	NA	NA
2007-08	24	12.56
2008-09	26	75
2009-10	28	79
2010-11	29	79.7

Source: Directorate of Horticulture, Govt. of Mizoram. NA-Not Acquired.

professional marketing skills and price speculation to avail the fruits of temporal price changes to the highly competitive domestic and international markets would be very risky and could end in farmers' distress, whatever the potential market opportunities may be. Fortunately, there are two organised marketing institutions/ stakeholders for anthurium flowers in Mizoram, though there is no market intervention scheme from the state government. They are Zopar Export Private Limited and Zo-Anthurium Growers Society.

1. *Zopar Exports Private Limited (ZEP).* A Bangalore-based Export Company named *Zopar Export Private Limited (ZEP)* was established on 3rd October, 2000 and is registered under Companies Registration Act, 1962. In Mizoram, ZEP has its main office in Chanmari, Aizawl while it hasanother retail outlet in Aizawl city, and one each in Kolasib and Lunglei towns. With the introduction of anthurium cultivation under Technology Mission scheme in Mizoram, ZEP had stepped out to facilitate the marketing of anthurium flowers, in addition to its normal flower business. It has become the main marketing agent till date. This firm usually sign buy-back agreement with the growers for their produce at a specified rate. After grading, packaging, and weighting the cut flowers it had collected (purchased) from the growers, the same are transported (by air) to its offices in Bangalore, Delhi, Kolkata, and Mumbai. The cut flowers received from Mizoram are sold to the retailers/consumers or exported to other countries from these offices. In addition to exporting the flowers to other states and countries, ZEP sells the flowers to the consumers from its main office and other retail outlets. Till June 2011, it had exported more than 27 lakh cut flowers of anthurium from Mizoram. The trend of annual export of anthurium flowers by ZEP since 2005 is presented in Table 3.16.

2. *Zo-Anthurium Growers Society (ZAGS).* Zo-Anthurium Growers Society was formed by a group of anthurium growers of Mizoram in 2004 and was registered under Societies Registration Act, 1976 on 17th September, 2004. It has its headquarters at Ramhlun Veng, Aizawl. The flowers collected from the society members are packaged, weighted, and graded at the headquarter office of ZAGS and is sent by air to an authorised retail agent in Delhi who is responsible for sale of all cut flowers received from Aizawl. This agent remitted the amount received from selling these

Table 3.16: Annual Export of Anthurium Flowers by Zopar Export Pvt. Ltd.

(In No. of Cut Flowers)

Year	*Mini*	*Semi-Medium (SM)*	*Medium (MD)*	*Large (L)*	*Extra Large (XL)*	*Jumbo (J)*	*Total*
2005	11357	14692	16272	9353	2060	149	53883
2006	53848	48272	42837	28481	6444	890	180772
2007	99033	121496	115286	87520	34054	7980	465369
2008	107157	210816	209673	142898	41670	17582	729796
2009	159766	223439	150266	89076	25544	12990	661081
2010	145002	164226	105809	61786	15811	8197	500831
2011*	27357	37784	32668	23194	6853	2981	130837
Total	603520	820725	672811	442308	132436	50769	2722569

Source: Zopar Export Private Limited, 2013.

* Till June 2011.

flowers to the ZAGS office at Aizawl, which would be distributed among the growers according to their quantity contribution. As such, there cannot be a fixed rate for flower procurement; it is rather directly linked with the sale performance of the agent in Delhi.

Market Channels

The existing marketing channels are determined by the two main marketing stakeholders in the state, viz. ZEP and ZAGS. The two differ in scope and coverage. While the ZEP can be accessed by producers if they are ready to sign pre-contract agreement in respect of procurement prices and terms of marketing, the scope of the latter (ZAGS) is restricted to members only. That is, members of ZAGS can market their commodities through either of the two, but the non-members can sell their produce only through ZEP or direct sale to local retailers/consumers. Considering all these aspects, the following market channels (Table 3.17) can be identified for anthurium flower in Mizoram.

If the flower brought by the growers to these agencies (ZEP & ZAGS) are not fit for export outside the state, the rejected cut flowers are disposed-off by the growers themselves in any way they can. At the same time, these growers also sell the flowers directly to the local consumer for use in church decorations,

Table 3.17: Marketing Channels of Anthurium Flowers in Mizoram

Channel – I	Producer – Consumer
Channel – II	Producer—Zopar Export Pvt. Ltd.—Export from the State—Market Terminals (Bangalore, Mumbai, Delhi and Kolkata)—Consumer/Export
Channel – III	Producer—ZAGS—Domestic Retailer (Delhi)—Consumer
Channel – IV	Producer—ZEP and ZAGS—Consumer (Local)

Figure 3.3: Flow Chart of Anthurium Marketing in Mizoram

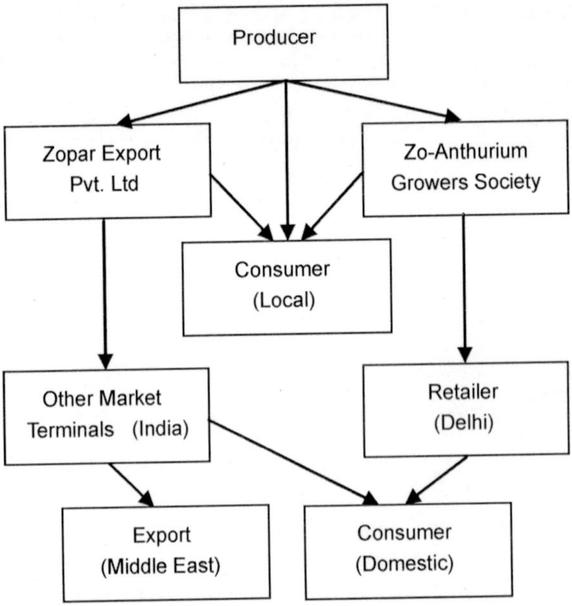

weddings, birthdays, etc. This is presented in Channel I. Second, the cases of flowers sold by the producers to ZEP, who processed it by grading, packing and weighting for onward export to big market terminals in other states, is given in Channel II. As mentioned earlier, these marketing agents would sell the commodity to domestic and export markets. Third, in Channel III is mentioned the members of ZAGS selling the flowers to its main office for onward export to Delhi, after packing, grading, and weighting. The agent in Delhi would market the same in the domestic market. Last, the offices of ZEP and ZAGS are operating as flower showroom and cut flowers are sold by these agencies directly to the local consumers. This is given in Channel IV.

Value Chain

Since the stakeholders interviewed during the course of data collection could not furnish the prices (whether in raw or processed form) of this commodity at the tertiary stage, the estimated value chain made in this section is based on the retail price of the flower obtained from *Okla Market*, New Delhi, which is known to be one of the main destinations of the flower produce of the State. At the same time, producer prices are different for various categories, viz. small, semi-medium, medium, large, extra-large, and jumbo, which changes during peak and off seasons. Considering all these conditions, it was decided to adopt median price to represent the prices of this commodity at different marketing stages. The use of median as an average price is theoretically acceptable as it rules out the possible effect of extreme values (very low or high) that may arise out of seasonal fluctuations.

In addition, the median retail price of cut flower at the local market is adopted as the value addition made by the local agent (ZEP), as they are not ready to reveal the rate of value addition they made for being the local facilitator who undertakes processing, packaging, transporting, etc. The estimated value chain of anthurium market among the various stakeholders is presented in Figure 3.4.

Figure 3.4: Estimated Value Chain for Anthurium Market Mizoram

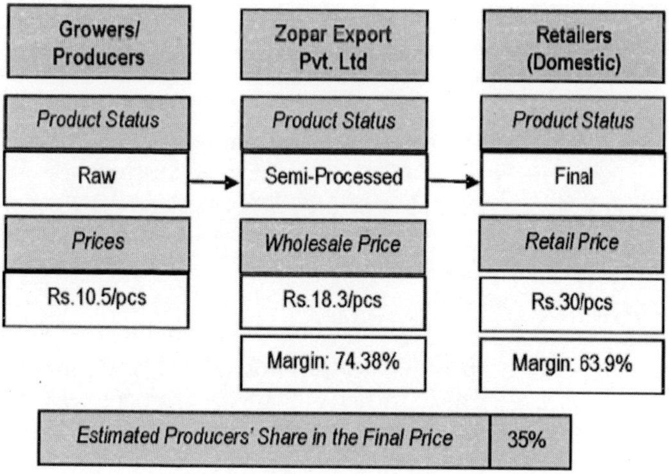

It can be observed from Figure 3.4 that the average procurement price of this commodity is Rs. 10.5 per piece; while the immediate market agent (ZEP) sell the same at the wholesale rate of Rs. 18.3 per piece, after packing, grading, and weighing for airlifting, to the market terminal located in Delhi who would sell it on retail. The structure of profit margin is another area of interest in this value chain. The estimated profit margin of ZEP is 74.38 per cent of the producer price, while the retailer's profit margin turned out to be 63.9 per cent of the wholesale price. Finally, the producer's share in the final price of the commodity is estimated to be 35 per cent. According to the interview of some knowledgeable persons, the prevailing producer's share in the final price could be augmented to great extent by providing better facilitative marketing infrastructure, like regular flight service, storage facilities, etc.

Seasonal Conditions in Anthurium Market

Knowledge of seasonal conditions of quantity arrivals and the corresponding prices are of crucial importance for marketing analysis. 'Season' should be of more importance for flower market than any other commodity because its demand is directly associated with community functions and festivals. Hence, its demand would increase during festive and wedding seasons (e.g. in India it starts in October and lasts till the coming of monsoon). At the same time, market efficiency depends on the responsiveness of prices to the quantity arrivals. The seasonal behaviour of anthurium flowers, as recorded by ZEP during the period of November 2010 till October 2011, is presented in Table 3.18.

Table 3.18 reveals an imbalance between the peak production and peak demand; that is, while the former starts with the onset of monsoon, the latter starts with dry season (i.e. November). In India, domestic market signal usually comes with the start of festive seasons in October which pressurised market prices. Accordingly, prices for different categories of cut flowers increase. Thus, the causal relationship between prices and quantity arrivals observed in this table suggests its implication on the operation of traditional economic theory.

Table 3.18: Indication of Seasonal Behaviour of Quantity Arrivals and Prices of Anthurium at Zopar Export Private Limited (During November 2010 to October 2011)

Prices (Rs/piece)							
Season	*Period*	*Small*	*Semi-Medium*	*Medium*	*Large*	*Extra Large*	*Jumbo*
Peak	May – October	2	3	8	9	10	11
Off	November - April	6	9	11	14	16	18
Quantity Arrival (No. of cut flowers)							
Peak	May – October	39312	51361	52703	38635	10937	4621
Off	November - April	26639	35827	25666	17654	4843	2309

Source: Zopar Export Private Limited, 2013.

Conclusion

There is lack of basic marketing infrastructure and institutions that would facilitate marketing of agricultural produce in Mizoram. The advantages of well-organised marketing institutions and channels have been indicated to result in higher producer's share in the final price, while the inverse is the case for unorganised market channels. Take, for example, the case of broom and areca-nut . The former is marketed through a well-organised marketing channel (i.e. HCP) and the latter is characterised by non-transparent and unorganised channels. The advantage of organised market channel is a relatively higher producer's share in the final price and earnings, and by generation of employment opportunities in the process of value addition by various stakeholders. At the same time, marketing of areca-nut shows unnecessary transit via Assam on account of intermediary intervention in its process resulting in low producer's share in the final price with the consumers being the losers as well. Public intervention scheme by encouraging and facilitating the emergence of organised marketing institutions in the state is of crucial importance to enhance the existing marketing chain and value addition. This would act as a counter-balance of the prices in open market.

In spite of it being grown largely across the State, ginger market is still characterised by unorganised and non-transparent channels. It shows complicated market channels with frequent intervention of intermediaries. Meanwhile, the state has been producing a substantial quantity as it produces, on an average, more than 30,000 metric tonnes every year. However, prices remain uncertain and the producers undertake risks in growing it. At the same time, any market intervention scheme put in place by the state government for ginger in the past was found ineffective and had adverse impact upon the procurement prices that prevailed in the open market. This has further unequivocally aggravated farmers' distress. Considering these experiences, one can conclude that any attempt made by the state government to directly interfere in markets is bound to fail. Thus, serious attention of the state government is invited to ensure regular dissemination of market (price) information to the producer for chalking out avenues for value addition and creating a congenial environment to attract private investment in the processing and marketing of ginger.

Shortage of storage facilities is another inhibiting factor towards the smooth flow of commodities market in the state. The farmers do not have the retaining capacity to wait for good marketing opportunities and to speculate prices in order to earn the profit of temporal price changes. In contrast, they have to dispose their produce as soon as they harvest it at whatever price and channel available. This, in turn, adversely affect the prevailing market price which result in farmer's loss due to low procurement prices that they could avoid had basic storage facilities been in place for them. Take for example the case of ginger. The peak harvesting period of ginger is December to March (Ref. Table 3.4). As against this, prices start to increase at the onset of monsoon season, May-June by which the farmers have to return to their cultivation fields. However, the unsold commodity harvested would be spoiled by then. Proper storage facility to store the commodity for at least two months would greatly enhance the earnings of the farmers.

Establishment of storage facilities and processing plants, like the ones being operated by traders in Assam, should be another area of interest to avoid unnecessary transit of areca-nut via Assam and frequent interface of the farmers with non-local commission agents. Any initiative to this end is expected to facilitate the emergence of a more organised areca-nut marketing channel and would motivate producers to produce more. As direct public intervention scheme usually fails (e.g. the case of ginger), encouragement of private investment in the matter is more suggestive.

Capacity development on the part of the growers to carry out the task of grading, packing, etc. of their produce would be another area of interest. Substantial amount (if not 100 percent) of the produce are sold by the farmers in unprocessed forms. There is a huge scope of enhancing their earnings by value addition, even by doing simple processing works. For example, the prevailing market rate of raw broom is Rs. 40 per kg, which would otherwise fetch around Rs. 100-150 if processed in its final form (broomsticks). Similarly, one piece of anthurium cut flower normally costs around Rs. 6-15; and as against this, a bouquet consisting of 6 to 15 pieces could fetch Rs. 350-500. These examples clearly indicate the possibility of increase in earnings of the growers through an enhancement of their capacity to process their own produce. Additionally, more employment opportunities would be generated in the process of value addition of agricultural produce in the state.

4

Marketing of Agriculture and Allied Products in the Local Market

This chapter covers fifteen agriculture and allied products sold in the local market of Mizoram which are obtained from different sources – within the state and imports. They are bean, brinjal, cabbage, green chilli, mustard leaf, tomato, garlic, onion, potato, turmeric, and fish, and fruits items like banana, lemon, orange, and pineapple. Though certain quantities of these commodities are exported outside the state, it is rather difficult to ascertain the quantities of such exports. Moreover, it is believed that major portion of the products are sold in the local market. A typical feature in the marketing of these commodities in Mizoram is that there is no known organised marketing channel and/or facilitating institution. Generally, farmers/producers sell their produce through whatever they deem profitable and is accessible to them, which makes it difficult to estimate the volume of quantity arrivals. In this chapter, therefore, more emphasis is given to the nature of marketing channels, price behaviour, and seasonal conditions.

Based on their nature and origin, the 15 commodities are classified into four categories as under:

Category-I	*Category-II*	*Category-III*	*Category-IV*
Bean	Fish	Pineapple	Garlic
Brinjal	Tomato	Orange	Onion
Cabbage		Lemon (Nimbu)	Potato
Green Chilli		Banana	Turmeric Powder
Mustard Leaf			

Local based vegetable items are clubbed under Category-I. The locally produced vegetables under this category constitute the major portion of the market flow in the state. Second, in Category-II are included the items in which the state mainly depends on import from outside, although certain amount of local produce is also marketed within the state. In Category-III is given fruit items. Significant portion of fruits being sold in the local market are known to have originated from within the state. Lastly, items which have regular market flow through a network of wholesale dealers and retailers are categorised under Category-IV. Items included in this category are mostly imported from outside, including imports from Myanmar, in either processed or semi-processed forms. Hence, the seasonal fluctuations of quantity arrivals for these commodities are mostly dependent on the condition of the means of road communication connecting the state.

Category – I (Bean, Brinjal, Cabbage, Green Chilli and Mustard Leaf)

Marketing Channels

As noted earlier, there is no organised marketing channel for the commodities of Category-I (Bean, Brinjal, Cabbage, Green Chilli and Mustard Leaf). They are characterised by unorganised networks of marketing agents. A peculiar feature of the market is that the producers themselves also act as retailers by directly selling their products to the final consumers. At the same time, a network of middlemen and wholesale commission agents play a crucial role in the marketing of these commodities as well. The whole system is very complicated that it is hard to identify the most frequented channel. The existing framework of marketing channel may be summarised in a flow chart as given in Figure 4.1.

The marketing channels that can be identified from Figure 4.1 are shown in Table 4.1. On the basis of the interview of various stakeholders, Channel III, IV, and V are the most common channels for marketing these commodities.

Broadly classified, there are four marketing agents. First, the *Producers* are the farmers who undertake cultivation of these food items in Jhum fields (*Tlang Lo*), and sometimes in WRC areas while rice is not cultivated (*Leilet*); settled rainfed areas (*Nul/Leipui*) and

Figure 4.1: Flow Chart of the Major Marketing Channels for Commodities under Category-I

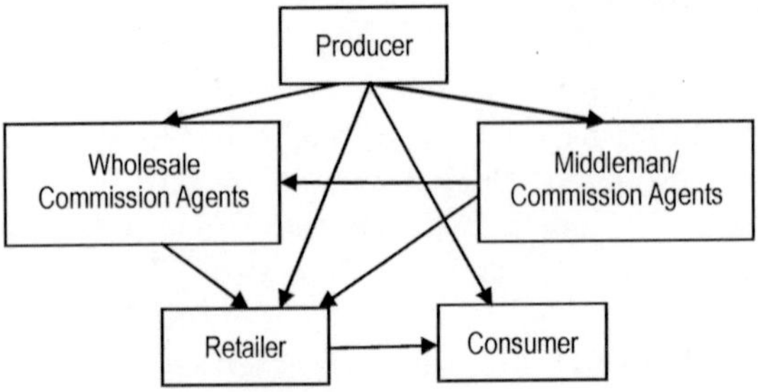

Table 4.1: Marketing Channels for Commodities (Category – I)

Channel I	Producer – Consumer
Channel II	Producer – Retailer – Consumer
Channel III	Producer – Wholesaler/ Wholesale Commission Agent – Retailer – Consumer
Channel IV	Producer – Middleman/Commission Agent – Wholesaler/ Wholesale Commission Agent – Retailer – Consumer
Channel V	Producer – Middleman/Commission Agent – Retailer – Consumer

in extended areas of homestead (*Chuktuah Huan*). Generally, these farmers sell their produce to middlemen or wholesale dealers who come to their villages in person or through a middleman. At the same time, there are some producers who transport their produce to market areas located in towns/the city (Aizawl), and sell them directly to consumers or retailers (vendors). These farmers usually go to the market place once a week, normally on a Saturday to avail the weekend bazaar. Distinctly called *'Mahni Thlaithar Zuar'* (Producer Sellers), they would sit alongside the main roads of the city/town and sell their products. They are given solicitude by the government as well as the people regarding their vending places because it is warranted as an incentive extended to the poor farmers of the state.

Second, *Wholesalers/Wholesale Commission Agents* are the traders who collect or procure commodities from the producers and sell it in bulk to the retailers who would further sell them to the consumers. They or their agents would go to different parts of the state to collect vegetables from farmers and then sell them to the retailers in the nearby town/city market places. As mentioned earlier in Chapter-1, members of the *'Mahni Thlai Zuar Association* (MTZA)' (Own Produce Vegetables Marketing Association) are the main actors. Though members of MTZA declare themselves to be producer farmers, they, in fact, act as wholesalers or as a link between producers and retailers.

Third, *Middlemen/Commission Agents* are marketing agents who act as a link between producers and wholesalers or retailers. They earn profit in the process of collection, storage, transportation and distribution of commodities. It may be noted that there are individuals in the villages who collect the surplus produce of the vegetables in their respective village for onward delivery to the wholesale dealers. Once sufficient quantity is collected, they would inform the wholesaler/agent to collect the commodities from the villages and in the process, earn a certain amount of commission fee. At the same time, some well-to-do families of the village or from other villages, who possess transport vehicles, collect these commodities from the villages and transport the same to sell them to retailers operating in urban areas at the prevailing wholesale prices thus earning certain amount of profit in the chain. These agents are also considered as middlemen.

Fourth, *Retailers* are the marketing agents who are in direct contact with the consumers. There are some instances where wholesalers are also involved in selling commodities directly to the consumers. Similarly, the producers are also selling their produce directly to the consumers by retailing it at the marketing areas. It is a common practice to market the products through any one of the above mentioned channels. Any market agent who has direct contact with the consumers can be identified as a retailer and his/her selling price as retail price.

Price Structure

One interesting feature of vegetable marketing in Mizoram is that, even though it is hard to factually determine organised marketing channels, there exists a more or less organised vegetable pricing in all the markets visited during the field work. Various associations of marketing agents were found to be at work that controls the prevailing vegetable price, which further depends on the supply conditions. It was also observed that there are vendor associations (like *Seling Bazar Thu Association*; *Thlai Thar Zuar*

Association of New Market, Aizawl; *Thlai Thar Zuar Association, Lunglei Bazar*; etc.) which in their attempt to check price competition among their members (which could end in loss) would set retail prices for commodities that had arrived in bulk from the wholesale commission agents. The usual practice is that these associations fix the minimum price for each item at the start of the day; but this limit is relaxed in the afternoon to enable distress sale by the petty vegetable vendors who are usually not facilitated with storage facilities. As such, vegetable prices are relatively high in the morning but are reduced in the evening in most of the markets.

Wholesalers also organise themselves in associations (like MTZA, etc.) to check price competition amongst themselves which could result in sustained profit for the members. It may be noted that as the prices for these commodities are set on an organised basis from producers to retailers, the various channels highlighted above do not show significant variations in each of the stages. That is, the retail prices in case of Channel I are more or less the same in other channels. This suggests that lower the number of agents in the marketing channel, the higher would be the producer's share in the final price.

Attempt is also made in this section to examine the value chain of these commodities based on prices recalled by marketing agents (wholesalers and retailers) of the selected market places. However, it is difficult to obtain quantity arrivals and the commissioning prices earned by the middlemen. The prices of these commodities tend to change every day and hence, only the average prices during the recalled period are presented. Nevertheless, the average prices are expected to reflect the true value chain for these commodities. Table 4.2 and Table 4.3 present the structure of price spread and profit margins among the various marketing agents.

The average producer price per kilogram (kg), across the study areas are Rs. 30, Rs. 24.44, Rs. 16, Rs. 28.33, and Rs. 11.25 for bean, brinjal, cabbage, green chilli, and mustard leaf, respectively. At the same time, the retailed prices for these commodities are Rs. 65, Rs. 38.33, Rs. 37.14, Rs. 136.43, and Rs. 50, respectively. The estimated transportation expenditure borne by the wholesalers or retailers to reach the market varies from Rs. 1.25 per kg in case of bean to Rs. 4 per kg for brinjal. The transportation expenditure, or marketing expenses, are added to the wholesale prices which is

Table 4.2: Price Spread of Vegetables (Category-I) among Various Stakeholders

Name of Vegetables	*Producer Price (Rs/Kg)*	*Whole-sale Price (Rs/Kg)*	*Estimated Transport Cost (Rs/kg)*	*CP of Retailers (incl. of Transport Cost) (Rs/Kg)*	*Retail Price (Rs/Kg)*	*Producer's Share in the Wholesale Price (%)*	*Producer's Share in the Final Price (%)*
Bean	30	48.75	1.25	50	65	61.54	46.15
Brinjal	24.44	28	4.00	32	38.33	87.30	63.77
Cabbage	16	22.43	1.76	20.67	37.14	71.34	43.08
Green Chilli	28.33	44.29	2.62	41.67	136.43	63.98	20.77
Mustard leaf	11.25	19.78	2.28	17.5	50	56.88	22.50

Source: Sample Survey, November 2013-January 2014.

Table 4.3: Structure of Profit Marginsearned by Various Stakeholders in the Marketing of Vegetables (under Category-I) in Mizoram

Name of Vegetables	*Wholesaler Price Margin (Rs./Kg)*	*Transportation Charges (Rs./Kg)*	*Retailers' Price (profit) Margin (Rs./Kg)*	*Wholesaler Profit (% of CP)*	*Transport Cost (% of Producers' Price)*	*Retailer Profit (% of CP)*
Bean	18.75	1.25	15.00	62.50	4.17	30.00
Brinjal	3.56	4.00	6.33	14.55	16.36	19.78
Cabbage	6.43	1.76	16.47	40.18	10.99	79.68
Green Chilli	15.95	2.62	94.76	56.30	9.23	227.41
Mustard Leaf	8.53	2.28	32.50	75.80	20.25	185.71

Source: Sample Survey, November 2013-January 2014.

then taken as actual cost price of the retailers. The commodities are usually packed in gunny/plastic bags and sent to market places through Maxi Cab Service or available transport services by paying the required carrying charge per pack/bag. Transportation expenditure per kilogram of these commodities is determined by dividing the amount paid per bag/packet by the total quantity.

Table 4.2 reveals that producer's share in the wholesale price ranges from 56.88 per cent in case of mustard leaf followed by bean with 61.54 per cent and 87.30 per cent in case of brinjal. Producer's share in the final price was found to be extremely low in case of green chilli (20.77 percent) and mustard leaf (22.50

percent), while it is slightly high for bean (46.15 percent) and cabbage (43.08 percent) though they are still less than 50 per cent. On the other hand, it is comparatively satisfactory for the case of brinjal (63.77 percent). Of the vegetables under this category, those that can be stored for relatively longer period ensured higher producer share (i.e. brinjal, bean, cabbage). The result presented in this table implicates the weak market influence of the producers for these commodities as only around 40 per cent (in average) of the final price is being pocketed by them. This suggests that the major portion of the final prices of vegetable produce and monetary benefits goes to the marketing actors (like wholesalers, middleman, retailers, etc.) and not to the producers.

Table 4.3 presents the profit margins of the main marketing agents of these commodities. Wholesaler's profit as a difference between wholesale price and producer's price is the highest in case of bean followed by green chilli, while it is the lowest in case of brinjal which shows the highest transportation cost per unit. On an average, the retail profit is higher than wholesale profit margins. That is, the retail profit ranges from Rs. 6.33 in case of brinjal to Rs. 94.76 in case of green chilli which is followed by mustard leaf (Rs. 32.50). It is a common practice among the retailers/vendors to split up a kilogram of certain commodities into a number of bundles or parts and charge prices for each of them. For example, 1 kg of green chilli (which is bought from the wholesalers at Rs. 28) is retailed in a full-cup measure and charged around Rs. 10 for a cup full of green chilli; and similarly, 1 kg of mustard leaf is divided into 2-3 bundles and sold at Rs. 10 per bundle; and so on. As such, the retailed profit margins for divisible commodities like green chilli and mustard leaf are relatively high.

Seasonal Conditions

Market arrivals and its prices are dependent upon the seasonal conditions of the commodities under study. Generally, prices tend to decline during peak season and increase during off season. Identification of the peak season and off season along with the corresponding changes in prices during these periods is crucial in formulating effective marketing policies. Table 4.4 presents the peak and off seasons of market arrivals for these commodities (Category-I). However, as the vegetable vendors and commission agents who operate their business without any proper record, are the sources of this information, we cannot rule out the possibility of committing errors. It may be noted here that peak and off seasons indicate peak period and off period of quantity arrivals. At the same time, Tables 4.5 and 4.6 presents seasonal variations of retail and wholesale prices for these commodities.

Table 4.4: Seasons of Market Arrivals for Bean, Brinjal, Cabbage, Green Chilli and Mustard Leaf in Mizoram.

<table>
<tr><th>Commodities</th><th>Jan</th><th>Feb</th><th>Mar</th><th>Apr</th><th>May</th><th>June</th><th>July</th><th>Aug</th><th>Sept</th><th>Oct</th><th>Nov</th><th>Dec</th></tr>
<tr><td>Bean</td><td>Peak</td><td></td><td></td><td></td><td colspan="3">Off</td><td></td><td></td><td></td><td colspan="2">Peak</td></tr>
<tr><td>Brinjal</td><td></td><td colspan="3">Off</td><td></td><td></td><td></td><td></td><td colspan="3">Peak</td><td></td></tr>
<tr><td>Cabbage</td><td></td><td colspan="2">Peak</td><td></td><td></td><td></td><td></td><td></td><td></td><td></td><td colspan="2">Off</td></tr>
<tr><td>Green Chilli</td><td></td><td></td><td></td><td></td><td colspan="3">Off</td><td></td><td colspan="4">Peak</td></tr>
<tr><td>Mustard Leaf</td><td>Peak</td><td></td><td colspan="3">Off</td><td></td><td></td><td></td><td></td><td></td><td colspan="2">Peak</td></tr>
</table>

Source: Sample Survey during November 2013 — January 2014.

Peak - Peak Season   Off -Off

Table 4.5: Seasonal Variations in the prices of Vegetables (Category-I) in Mizoram: Based on the Cross Sectional Data of Retailers

Rs/Kg

Prices Status	*Season*	*Price Range*	*Bean*	*Brinjal*	*Cabbage*	*Green Chilli*	*Mustard Leaf*
Wholesale Prices	Peak	Min	30	16	8	33	11
		Max	48	26	15	46	20
		Average	**39**	**21**	**12**	**39**	**16**
	Off	Min	62	34	24	65	25
		Max	82	49	32	85	36
		Average	**72**	**42**	**28**	**75**	**31**
Retail Prices	Peak	Min	51	23	15	47	19
		Max	66	36	23	65	32
		Average	**59**	**30**	**19**	**56**	**25**
	Off	Min	83	53	34	85	36
		Max	106	69	45	109	51
		Average	**95**	**61**	**39**	**97**	**44**

Source: Sample Survey during November 2013 – January 2014.

Table 4.5 and 4.6 presents the trend of low prices (wholesale and retail) during the period of peak and high prices during off period. On average, retail prices are significantly higher in each of the period, as also for the two periods taken together. The difference between them represents retail profit. Taking the two seasons together, retail profit ranges from 34 per cent of the wholesale price in case of green chilli to 49 per cent for cabbage and mustard leaf. Another interesting feature is that the average retail profit per kg of the commodity is higher during peak arrival period than during off seasons for all commodities, except for brinjal.

Spatial Allocation of Marketable Surplus

The commodities in this category are, in fact, the main vegetable items consumed by the people of the state since early times. They are cultivated in Jhum land and extended areas of homestead. As they are consumed everywhere in the state, most of the villages in rural areas grow these crops at least for their own consumption. Therefore, the existence of surplus production, which do not reach the big market places but are marketed in the village, cannot be ruled out either. Taking this into account, it is a difficult task to locate the areas concentrated in cultivating these items at substantial volumes and those that have surplus production for marketing at other places.

It is generally accepted that these commodities, irrespective of its quantity, could be grown and produced anywhere across the state in which Jhumming is practised. Whatever the case, the state has not been able to produce enough quantity of these commodities especially during their off seasons and has to import them from outside sources. Attempt is made in this section to identify the main feeders of the sampled market places covered during the field work (Table 4.7).

One interesting feature that can be derived from Table 4.7 is that Aizawl bazaar continues to be the main source of market arrivals among all the markets in the state. Traders in Aizawl market, in turn, import the items from outside the state whenever there is insufficiency in local supply to meet demand, and when the prices of such imports are uncompetitive. These commodities, in turn, are passed on to other market areas. As these items can be produced in almost any part of the state, there is a huge scope for increasing its production, which if assisted with the prevalence of well-organised marketing channels and basic infrastructure, could prove highly beneficial.

Table 4.6: Changes in the Retail Profit Margins of Vegetables Marketing (Category-I) in Peak and Off Seasons: Based on the Cross Sectional Data of Retailers

Rs/Kg

Seasons	*Particulars*	*Bean*	*Brinjal*	*Cabbage*	*Green Chilli*	*Mustard Leaf*
Peak Season	Average Wholesale Price	39	21	12	39	16
	Average Retail Price	59	30	19	56	25
	Retail Profit Margin	20	9	8	17	10
	Retail Profit Margin (%)	51	42	66	43	64
Off Season	Average Wholesale Price	72	42	28	75	31
	Average Retail Price	95	61	39	97	44
	Retail Profit Margin	22	19	12	22	13
	Retail Profit Margin (%)	31	45	42	30	42
All Seasons	Average Wholesale Price	55	31	20	57	23
	Average Retail Price	77	45	29	77	35
	Retail Profit Margin	21	14	10	19	11
	Retail Profit Margin (%)	38	44	49	34	49

Source: Sample Survey during November 2013 - January 2014.

Table 4.7: Feeders of Vegetables (Category-I) of the Selected Market Places in Mizoram

Market Place	*Main Sources (Feeders)*
Aizawl	Sihphir, Durtlang, Lungdai, Sairang, Maite, Tuirini, Keifang, Sesawng, Tualbung, Saitual, Samlukhai, Thiak, Zawlpui, Thingsulthliah, Mualpheng, Dilkhan; Assam, Meghalaya, Myanmar
Seling	Sihphir, Aizawl bazar, Tuirnini, Maite, Sihfa, Tuirial, Seling, Thingsulthliah, Tualbung, Mualpheng
Champhai	Champhai, Ruantlang, Dilkawn, Zote, Tuipui, Zotlang, Hmunhmeltha, Leisenzo, Mualkawi, Aizawl Bazar, Myanmar
Serchhip	Serchhip, Zawlpui, Sihphir, Durtlang, Khawlailung, Sialsir, Aizawl Bazar, Hriangtlang
Lunglei	Aizawl Bazar, Tuichawng, Tlabung, Sihphir, Durtlang, Hauruang, Theiriat, Pukpui, Zawlpui, Phairuangkai, Tuipui D, Leite, Ralvawng
Saiha	Aizawl Bazar, Lungdai, Sihphir, Bualpui S, Cheural, Theiva, Siachangkawn, S. Lungpher, Vawmbuk

Category – II (Fish and Tomato)

Overview of Production

The two commodities included in this category are those, among the selected 20 items, in which the state has been depending on imports from outside the state. They are sold in the main bazaars by small vendors or retailers. Though they are also produced within the state, the quantity of imports contribute the major portion throughout the year. In spite of it being imported regularly from other states, there is no official record of it during the last many years. Hence, it is not possible to estimate the contribution of outside sources on the total quantity arrivals in the local market. Further, the agents (retailers and commission agents) contacted did not have clear knowledge about the origin and chain of value addition. Therefore, we would try to present in this section a brief outline of its marketing and other relevant marketing information.

Table 4.8 presents the expansion of area and production of fish and tomato in Mizoram. It can be observed that area under fish farming increased from 2580 hectares in 2005-06 to 4075.6 hectares in 2011-12. With the adoption of fisheries/pisciculture as one of the activities of NLUP, being implemented in the state from 2011, the area is expected to increase further. Production also increased to a great extent from 3750 metric tonnes in 2005-06 to 5113.02 metric tonnes in 2011-12.

Table 4.8: Area and Production of Fish and Tomato in Mizoram

Year	*Fish*		*Tomato*	
	Area (Ha)	*Production (MT)*	*Area (Ha)*	*Production (MT)*
2005-06	2580.00	3750.00	16	274
2006-07	2597.35	3758.55	17	225
2007-08	2875.40	2764.65	17	298
2008-09	3802.80	3624.41	620	4960
2009-10	3953.80	4136.56	NA	NA
2010-11	3978.00	4621.40	675	6075
2011-12	4075.60	5113.02	700	6420

Source: Statistical Handbook of Mizoram 2012, Statistical Abstract of Mizoram, 2009 and http://fisheries.mizoram.gov.in

Area under tomato cultivation and production also increased significantly during the seven years under study. The area increased from a mere 16 hectares in 2005-06 to 700 hectares in 2011-12. At the same time, production also increased from 274 metric tonnes to 6420 metric tonnes during the same period. The state saw a significant leap in the case of area under cultivation and production for this commodity following its inclusion under Technology Mission since the fiscal year 2006-07. This Mission aimed at increasing the production of some horticultural crops like flowers, tomato, etc. At the same time, an analysis of the information obtained from various sources casted doubt on the quantity of local production as recorded in the official data. This is due to the fact that major portion of the commodity sold in the local market is constituted by import from outside sources. As such, it may not be safe to rely on the official record of tomato production in Mizoram.

District-wise data on the production and area coverage, given in Table 4.9, shows that almost 60 per cent of fish production in the state is contributed by Mamit and Kolasib districts. Further, the major portions of the low lying areas of the state are in these two districts which are bounded by the states of Assam and Tripura. Due to favourable landscape and accessibility to outside market opportunities, fish farming has prevailed in these areas since long time back.

Table 4.9: District-Wise Area and Production of Fish in Mizoram during 2012-13

District	*Total No. of Farmers*	*Total Area (Ha)*	*Production (MT)*	*Total No. of Farmers (%)*	*Total Area (%)*	*Production (%)*
Mamit	1826	995.3	1492.95	16.85	22.29	28.44
Kolasib	2110	1035.2	1552.8	19.47	23.18	29.58
Aizawl	1167	290.9	276.355	10.77	6.52	5.26
Champhai	1085	303.4	303.4	10.01	6.80	5.78
Serchhip	857	226.3	226.3	7.91	5.07	4.31
Lunglei	1446	550.2	440.16	13.34	12.32	8.39
Lawngtlai	1526	699.2	629.28	14.08	15.66	11.99
Saiha	821	364.5	328.05	7.58	8.16	6.25
TOTAL	10838	4465	5249.295	100	100	100

Source: http://fisheries.mizoram.gov.in

Marketing Channels

(a) Fish sold in Mizoram are from two main sources—local and imports from outside. Normally, the local fish is harvested during the dry season of the year starting from November which lasts till March. Local fish products are marketed through two main channels: export to Assam and local market sale. At the time of harvesting, individuals from Assam would come to the village and collect the bigger sized fish from the producers at quoted (and bargained) prices of the farmers. The fish are usually priced according to their size and not in kilograms. The agents would then transport the procured fish to market areas in Assam and sell them singly to the highest bidder. It was reported (but not verified) that fish bought from Mizoram are in high demand in these areas, so much so that there cannot be a clear and precise rate for the different sizes because they are sold on auction basis.

The remaining smaller-sized fish that could not be sold to these non-local agents are being sold to the local commission agents who transport it to towns and the city for retail sales. Since there is no available cold storage van to transport the fish to other locations, these agents are obliged to buy ice blocks from ice plants operated by the government to keep the fish from being spoiled in the transportation process. There are also instances in which the producers themselves sell their produce directly to the consumers at different urban areas of the state. Figure 4.2 presents the usual channels of fish market in Mizoram.

Figure 4.2: Flow Chart Indicating the Marketing Channel of Fish in Mizoram

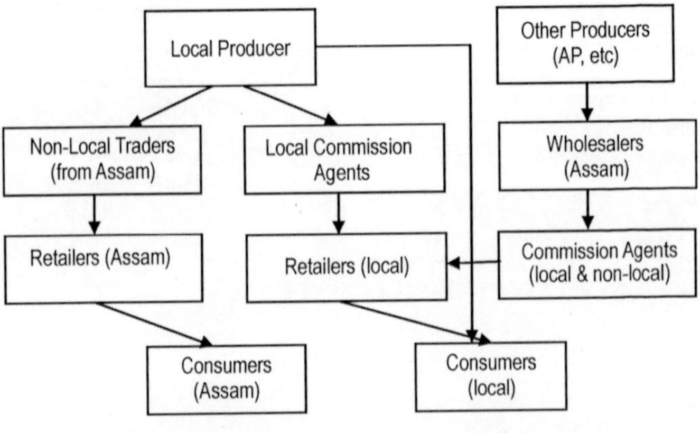

Since the supply of local fish in the market is in periodic intervals, i.e. especially during winter season, local demand has to be catered by import from other states. As per the record of the agents contacted during the field work, substantial quantity (if not the main portion) of the state's import of fish originates from the state of Andhra Pradesh (AP). It was reported that wholesalers dealing in Silchar area of Assam purchase the commodity from AP and delivers it to the local or non-local commission agents operating in the state for onward sale to the retail dealers. Due to lack of proper storage facilities in the state, these wholesale dealers would deliver only the quantity of order placed by the commission agents. The quantity demanded by the commission agent is determined by their anticipation of market demand in Mizoram. Moreover, since these agents had experienced that storing the produce in the cold storage run by the Fishery Department is unaffordable and practically inaccessible, they prefer to store it with ice blocks purchased from the state run ice plants to prevent it from spoilage.

It may be noted that the state government's Fishery Department aims at improving the fish marketing network of the state with hope of an even distribution of the harvested fish to major markets and in the interior areas of the state. It has installed one ice plant-cum-cold storage each in at Bawngkawn and Kolasib, and one ice plant at Bilkhawthlir. Reportedly, these plants are running successfully in providing quality ice blocks, cold storage facility, etc. to the fish farmers/sellers at subsidised rate for preservation and marketing of fishes. At the same time, the farmers are also assisted with the provision of ice boxes and plastic crates for storing the harvested fish.

(b) There are three main sources of tomato sold in the local markets, namely, local products, import from other states, and import from Myanmar. Of these sources, import from other states constitute the major portion of market arrivals in Mizoram, while the remaining two sources also contribute substantial amount as well. Though it is very hard to determine the origin of the produce, local commission agents were found to be playing a major role in its marketing. The flow chart given in Figure 4.3 presents the main market channel of tomato in Mizoram.

Figure 4.3: Flow chart Indicating the Marketing Channel of Tomato in Mizoram

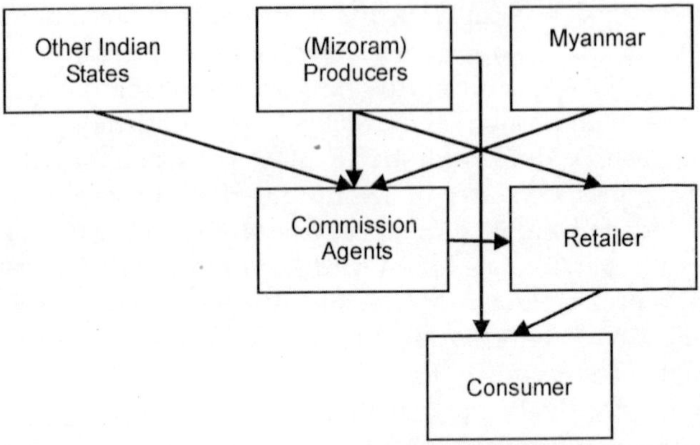

It can be observed from Figure 4.3 that commission agents (local and non-local) are playing a major role in the marketing of tomato in Mizoram, especially for the imported ones. Tomatoes imported from other states of India like Meghalaya, Assam, etc. are being delivered to the local retailers by the intermediaries (here called commission agents), who would sell them at retail prices. At the same time, although there is no formal trade between India and Myanmar for marketing vegetables, substantial quantity of tomato is being (unofficially) imported regularly from Myanmar through the border village of Zokhawthar (Champhai). Local commission agents would go to the border and purchase the commodity and then transport it to retailers at different parts of the state. In addition to imports from other states and Myanmar, farmers in the state also produce tomatoes and sell their produce either directly to the consumers or to the commission agents or the retailers.

Marketing Seasons and Value Chain

Since there are two sources for these products—local and outside sources, there are, more or less, uninterrupted market arrivals in all markets throughout the year. The seasons (peak or off) for these commodities as identified in the survey is given in Table 4.10. However, the seasons presented in this table are subject to change on account of variation in the supply from outside sources, which is difficult to forecast. The peak season for the two commodities starts with the coming of dry season; while the off season starts at the onset of monsoon.

Table 4.10: Seasonal Conditions for Quantity Arrivals of Fish and Tomato in Mizoram

<table>
<tr><th>Items</th><th>Jan</th><th>Feb</th><th>Mar</th><th>Apr</th><th>May</th><th>June</th><th>Jul</th><th>Aug</th><th>Sept</th><th>Oct</th><th>Nov</th><th>Dec</th></tr>
<tr><td>Fish</td><td colspan="2">Peak</td><td></td><td></td><td></td><td colspan="3">Off</td><td></td><td></td><td></td><td>Peak</td></tr>
<tr><td>Tomato</td><td colspan="3">Peak</td><td></td><td></td><td></td><td colspan="3">Off</td><td></td><td></td><td></td></tr>
</table>

Source: Sample Survey during November 2013–January 2014.

Peak - Peak Season Off - Off Season

The price structure in each of the seasons and profit margins of the retailers are presented in Table 4.11 and 4.12. Due to insufficient price information, the prices that the retailers pay to immediate dealers (i.e. commission agents or wholesalers) are simply adopted as wholesale price, and the difference between retail price and wholesale price represent retail margin (or retail profit margin) for that commodity.

As expected, prices tend to increase as we move from peak to off season. On an average, the retail profit margin is higher in case of fish when compared with tomato. The average retail profit margin for fish is 28.87 per cent of the wholesale price, while it is 23.94 per cent for tomato for the two seasons taken together. Higher retail profit margin being observed in case of fish may be due to the arrival of locally produced fish in the market which fetch higher prices than imported ones. This has pulled up the average (or median) retail price resulting in higher average profit margin.

Category – III (Orange, Banana, Pineapple, and Lemon)

Production and Cultivation

Commodities considered in this section are the major fruits items (Orange, Banana, Pineapple, and Lemon) produced and consumed in Mizoram. They are produced in huge quantities and it appears that there is a potential for the state to be self-sufficient in its production. In fact, the state has been exporting orange to other states since long time back. The production and areas under

Table 4.11: Retail Price Margins Fish and Tomato in Mizoram

Seasons	*Particulars*	*Fish*	*Tomato*
Peak Season	Average Wholesale Price (Rs/Kg) Average Retail Price (Rs/Kg) Retail Profit Margin (Rs/Kg) Retail Profit Margin (%)	125 175 50 41.67	131 162 31 23.58
Off Season	Average Wholesale Price (Rs/Kg) Average Retail Price (Rs/Kg) Retail Profit Margin (Rs/Kg) Retail Profit Margin (%)	160 190 30 18.75	149 185 36 24.26
All Seasons	Average Wholesale Price (Rs/Kg) Average Retail Price (Rs/Kg) Retail Profit Margin (Rs/Kg) Retail Profit Margin (%)	142 183 41 28.87	140 174 34 23.94

Source: Sample Survey during November 2013—January 2014.

Table 4.12: Seasonal Variations in the Prices of Fish and Tomato in Mizoram

Prices Status	*Season*	*Price Range*	*Fish*	*Tomato*
Wholesale Prices	Peak	Min Max Average	110 140 125	26 30 131
	Off	Min Max Average	140 180 160	49 69 149
Retail Prices	Peak	Min Max Average	150 200 175	40 50 162
	Off	Min Max Average	160 220 190	70 88 185

Source: Sample Survey during November 2013 - January 2014.

cultivation of these fruit items have increased tremendously during the last ten years. This is presented in Table 4.13.

As the climatic condition of the state is favourable for the cultivation of these fruits, there is huge scope for expanding their area under cultivation and their production. With the implementation of NLUP in the state, large number of families has taken up fruit cultivation since 2011. For instance, the record of the state government shows that 4,396 families adopted orange

Table 4.13: Area and Production of the 4 Selected Fruit Items in Mizoram

Year	Orange		Banana		Pineapple		Lemon (Nimbu)	
	Area (Ha)	Production (MT)	Area (Ha)	Production (MT)	Area (Ha)	Production (MT)	Area (Ha)	Production (MT)
2002-03	5429	25050	2734	44564	777	2685	778	1739
2010-11	7682	19700	10639	118600	2260	13590	4996	24150
2011-12	8360	22230	10090	119060	2720	19650	4850	24710

Source: Statistical Handbook of Mizoram 2004 and Economic Survey of Mizoram, 2012-13.

cultivation during 2011-12 and another 4,500 families spreading across the state were expected to adopt the same during 2013-14 under the state's flagship programme of NLUP. Similarly, an additional number of around 3000 families were expected to take up pineapple cultivation under the same scheme during 2013-14. Thus, the existing trend indicates production of substantial amount of these fruit items in the state in the next few years. This scenario entails a notion that it is a high time to think about and put forth a strategy for post-harvest management and marketing of these items.

Market Channels

With the exception of orange, the fruits produced in the state are sold solely in the local market. These fruits are marketed in both unprocessed and processed (or semi-processed) form in the local market. Middlemen occupy a prominent place in the marketing of fruit items in Mizoram. They are the individuals who would go to different villages to collect the produce and later transport them and sell it to the retailers. At the same time, the farmers themselves also sell their produce directly to consumers in their respective areas or to retailers dealing in other places by hiring transport vehicles. The normal market channels of fruits items in Mizoram are presented in Figure 4.4.

First, a notable feature of pineapple marketing in the state is the role played by Mizoram Food and Allied Industries Corporation Limited (MIFCO), a Government of Mizoram undertaking. This corporation collects the product from the farmers either directly or through middlemen/collectors and

Figure 4.4: Flow Chart Indicating the Marketing Channels of Pineapple, Lemon, Banana and Orange in Mizoram

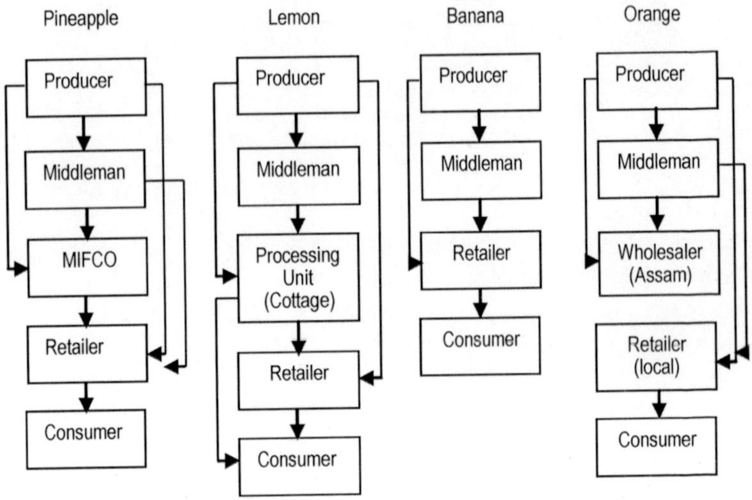

process it to its final form at the processing plant in Chhingchhip, Serchhip district, Mizoram. Substantial quantities of locally produced pineapples are processed in the plant and the final products are marketed in different retail outlets of MIFCO in the state. Meanwhile, marketing of the unprocessed fruits also occupy an important place. The producers sell their produce to retail dealers directly or through middlemen for onward sale to consumers. It may be noted that import of this commodity from other states, like Lakhimpur in the state of Assam, have also contributed a significant percentage of quantity arrivals in the local market.

Second, the locally produced lemon (called 'nimbu' in local dialect) is also marketed in two forms—unprocessed and processed (juice). There are some Mizo traders engaged in the extraction of lemon juice using homemade tools who sells them to the consumers directly or indirectly through retailers. These individuals collect the unprocessed lemon from the farmers or middlemen and process it. At the same time, selling of lemon in its unprocessed form occupies a prominent place in the local market. Third, banana also reaches the consumer through the two main agents of middlemen and retailers.

Fourth, there are two main marketing venues for orange in the state, namely local and export markets. The main actor in this channel is again a middleman, local or non-local, who purchase the commodity from the farmers and transport it to other places. It was reported that major portion of the produce is being sold outside the state through these middlemen. After being purchased and kept in storage arrangements at other states, certain amount is again bought back from outside the state by local retailers during off seasons. Further, there is a huge marketing opportunity at other parts of the country for this product.

Selling of orange to non-local middlemen (commission agents) by the farmers is done in two ways: (i) Before the start of harvesting season, these agents, normally from Assam, would come to the village to commission the orange on tree basis at agreed prices between the producers and themselves; (ii) When the producers have harvested the fruit, the commission agents would come to collect the commodity by paying the price quoted by the producers. These agents transport the same to big wholesale dealers in other states (Assam) for further processing. At the same time, some local middlemen (businessmen) also sell the commodity to the retailers operating in different market stations within the state; while some producers themselves prefer to deliver it directly to the retailers in the market places, especially in urban areas of the state.

Market Seasons and Origin

The marketing seasons of the four items under study can broadly be classified into two—dry season and wet (monsoon) season. The peak period for orange and banana occur during dry period, while the off season starts with the coming of monsoon. At the same time, peak period for market arrivals in case of pineapple and lemon occurs during the wet season (monsoon). The periodic conditions of the four fruit items are presented in Table 4.14. This study observed that the state's geo-climatic condition is favourable for the successful cultivation of these fruits items. This is indicated by the analysis of the sources of these items which are scattered at different parts of the state.

Table 4.14: Seasons of Market Arrivals for Fruits (Category-III) in Mizoram

<table>
<tr><th>Commodities</th><th>Jan</th><th>Feb</th><th>Mar</th><th>Apr</th><th>May</th><th>June</th><th>July</th><th>Aug</th><th>Sept</th><th>Oct</th><th>Nov</th><th>Dec</th></tr>
<tr><td>Pineapple</td><td></td><td></td><td></td><td></td><td></td><td colspan="3">Peak</td><td></td><td colspan="3">Off</td></tr>
<tr><td>Orange</td><td colspan="2">Peak</td><td></td><td></td><td colspan="3">Off</td><td></td><td></td><td></td><td></td><td>Peak</td></tr>
<tr><td>Lemon (Nimbu)</td><td></td><td colspan="3">Off</td><td></td><td colspan="4">Peak</td><td></td><td></td><td></td></tr>
<tr><td>Banana</td><td colspan="3">Peak</td><td></td><td></td><td></td><td colspan="3">Off</td><td></td><td></td><td>Peak</td></tr>
</table>

Source: Sample Survey during November 2013 – January 2014

Peak - Peak Season Off - Off Season

Price Structure

The price structure of the fruits that prevail in the market areas covered in the survey are presented in Table 4.15 and 4.16. As before, we adopt the prices at which the retailers purchase the commodity from the immediate market agent (middlemen, etc.) as wholesale prices; and the difference between wholesale price and retail price as retail (profit) margins. Further, while lemon is priced per kg, the remaining items are priced on a per piece basis.

The prices of these products tend to increase during off season for market arrivals, while it decreases during peak period. The average retail profit margin as a percentage of wholesale price is higher side than the commodities of the other categories. All seasons' retail profit margins ranged from 52.47 per cent in case of lemon to 70.62 per cent for banana. This denotes the viability of fruit market and better opportunities for expansion and value addition in the state.

Category – IV (Potato, Onion, Garlic, and Turmeric)

Production and Area under Cultivation

Agricultural products in which the state depends heavily on outside sources and in which the local market is being dominated by such imports are included in this section. Unlike other commodities covered in the survey, which are sold mainly by vegetable vendors in the bazaars, these commodities are usually

Table 4.15: Retail Price Margins of Selected Fruit Items in Mizoram

Seasons	*Particulars*	*Pine-apple (Rs/pcs)*	*Orange (Rs/pcs)*	*Lemon (Rs/Kg)*	*Banana (Rs/pcs)*
Peak Season	Average Wholesale Price	19.17	3.83	12.05	2.61
	Average Retail Price	31.95	6.88	21.04	4.59
	Retail Profit Margin	12.78	3.05	8.99	1.98
	Retail Profit Margin (%)	66.67	79.63	74.61	75.86
Off Season	Average Wholesale Price	36.39	6.36	24.77	4.46
	Average Retail Price	56.11	10.38	35.09	7.48
	Retail Profit Margin	19.72	4.02	10.32	3.02
	Retail Profit Margin (%)	54.19	63.21	41.66	67.71
All Seasons	Average Wholesale Price	27.78	5.1	18.41	3.54
	Average Retail Price	44.03	8.63	28.07	6.04
	Retail Profit Margin	16.25	3.53	9.66	2.5
	Retail Profit Margin (%)	58.50	69.22	52.47	70.62

Source: Sample Survey, November 2013 – January 2014. Note pcs – piece

Table 4.16: Seasonal Variations in the Prices of Selected Fruit Items in Mizoram

Type of Price	*Season*	*Range*	*Pineapple (Rs/pcs)*	*Orange (Rs/pcs)*	*Lemon (Rs/Kg)*	*Banana (Rs/pcs)*
Wholesale Price	Peak	Min	16.11	3.08	8.55	2.04
		Max	22.22	4.58	15.55	3.17
		Average	**19.17**	**3.83**	**12.05**	**2.61**
	Off	Min	31.67	5.46	20.09	3.75
		Max	41.11	7.25	29.45	5.17
		Average	**36.39**	**6.36**	**24.77**	**4.46**
Retail Price	Peak	Min	27.22	5.5	15.36	3.75
		Max	36.67	8.25	26.72	5.42
		Average	**31.95**	**6.88**	**21.04**	**4.59**
	Off	Min	47.78	8.92	28.82	6.54
		Max	64.44	11.83	41.36	8.42
		Average	**56.11**	**10.38**	**35.09**	**7.48**

Source: Sample Survey, November 2013 - January 2014. Note pcs – piece.

sold by various shops/retailers and wholesalers in different parts of the state.

Table 4.17 presents the progress of production and cultivation area of potato and turmeric in the state.

Table 4.17: Area and Production of Potato and Turmeric in Mizoram

Year	*Potato*		*Turmeric*	
	Area (Ha)	*Production (MT)*	*Area (Ha)*	*Production (MT)*
2000-01	310	2429	NA	NA
2001-02	376	1472	280	2808
2002-03	369	726	287	3845
2003-04	363	893	320	4528
2004-05	504	2531	385	5509
2005-06	953	3891	522	9735
2006-07	639	1652	535	10074
2007-08	330	1158	4175	83500
2008-09	269	1569	9625	39862
2009-10	150	2090	4500	22500
2010-11	200	2300	4780	23900

Source: Various Issues of Economic Survey of Mizoram and Statistical Abstract of Mizoram 2009, Directorate of Economics and Statistics, Government of Mizoram

Some farmers of the state started extensive cultivation of turmeric with its inclusion under the centrally sponsored state project named Technology Mission since 2007. Local products of turmeric in processed form, i.e. turmeric powder, have started coming to the local market alongside the imported ones. At the same time, expansion of production and area under cultivation is not found in case of potato in Mizoram. In respect of onion and garlic, there is no local produce to be found in the market nor are there any official record of their production and cultivation.

Product Origins and Marketing Channels

We can broadly classify the commodities included in Category-IV into two—imported from Indian state (including local source) and those imported from other states and neighbouring countries. Potato and turmeric belong to the former, while onion and garlic belong to the latter. Wholesalers or wholesale dealers occupy a prominent place in the marketing of the four commodities. The existing market channels for these commodities are presented in Figure 4.5.

First, the major sources of potato are the states of Meghalaya and West Bengal. Imports from Meghalaya usually start from August till the end of December; while imports of the latter starts

Figure 4.5: Flow Chart indicating the market channels of Potato, Turmeric, Onion and Garlic, Onion and Garlic in Mizoram

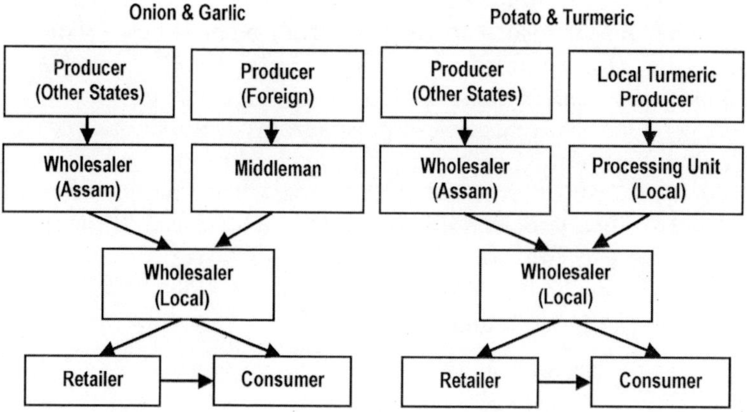

from January and lasts till August. It is safe to say that almost all the potato produce sold and bought in the market are from other states. It was observed that there are two stages of wholesale dealing before reaching the retailers. The product whether from Meghalaya or West Bengal, is firstly obtained by wholesalers operating in Assam, and these agents would then deliver the commodity to the local wholesale agents. The local wholesale agent place the quantity order to these wholesalers, and the latter would supply the same to the former. Further, local wholesalers were also found to be selling potatoes directly to the consumers at the prevailing retail prices, in addition to their wholesale sale to retailers.

Second, there are two major sources of turmeric powder marketed in the local market, namely local products and import from other states. It may be noted that extensive cultivation of turmeric in the state started from the last few years. To facilitate its cultivators, the state government set up a turmeric processing plant in Reiek village to cater to the need of turmeric growers in this cluster. This is denoted in the channels (Figure 4.5) as local processing plant. The product of this processing plant is being sold in the local market. At the same time, turmeric powder imported from other states still occupies the major portion of the product being marketed in the state.

Third, roughly more than 70 per cent of the onion sold in the local market is contributed by imports from other states of India through wholesalers dealing in and around Silchar, Assam. The state also import from the neighbouring country of Myanmar as and when there is insufficient supply from other states. At the same time, the demand for Myanmar-produced garlic is comparatively high because its cloves are bigger compared to India's produce. As such, garlic imported from Myanmar occupies more than half of the product sold in the local market, which is followed by import from other states and from Bangladesh. Imported items are mostly obtained by the wholesalers through middlemen (or commission agents) operating along the international border of Myanmar (Zokhawthar, Champhai) and Bangladesh (Tlabung, Lunglei District).

Cost Structure

It is unfortunate to note that marketing agents (mainly wholesalers) contacted during the field work were not ready to provide reliable information on the structure of prices and market chain. Moreover, they do not keep proper records of (or are not willing to show) their transaction even for the last few months, and were not clear about the seasonal conditions for quantity arrivals in the local market. What can be obtained is a rough estimate only. The structure of cost and selling prices at the wholesale and retail dealing stages are, as obtained from the survey of some business establishments in the state, presented in Table 4.18 and 4.19.

Interestingly, the reported selling prices of wholesalers are slightly higher than the cost price of retailers for all cases. This has suggested the presence of marketing costs in the form of transportation expenses, etc. The average profit margins, as a percentage of cost price, at the two stages (wholesale and retail) are low compared with other items enumerated in this chapter. The overall profit margin ranged from 15.33 per cent in case of turmeric powder to 21.07 per cent for potato. Moreover, a reasonable assumption that could be made is that the commodities included in this category are final or at least in semi-processed forms and hence, the stakeholders have the needed storage capacity in spite of the absence of further facilities. Thus, the marketing of these commodities do not entail elements of rush or distress sale, which is usually done to avoid commodity spoilage, of the degree of the other agricultural products studied in the survey.

Table 4.18: Cost Structure of Garlic, Onion, Potato and Turmeric Powder in Mizoram

Rs/Kg

Dealer Status	*Season*	*Range*	*Garlic*	*Onion*	*Potato*	*Turmeric Powder*
Wholesaler	Cost Price	Min	68.13	19.8	8.94	180
		Max	97.5	62.09	26.86	203
		Average	**82.82**	**40.95**	**17.90**	**191.5**
	Selling Price	Min	75.56	25.14	10.22	200
		Max	110.75	75.03	30.61	222
		Average	**93.16**	**50.09**	**20.42**	**211**
Retailer	Cost Price	Min	77.3	25.81	10.25	203.6
		Max	113	75.19	31.2	230
		Average	**95.15**	**50.5**	**20.73**	**216.8**
	Selling Price	Min	100	32.22	13.2	248.6
		Max	140	86.07	39.5	270
		Average	**120**	**59.15**	**26.35**	**259.30**

Source: Market Survey during November 2013 – January 2014.

Table 4.19: Retail Profit Marginsin the Marketing of Garlic, Onion, Potato and Turmeric Powder in Mizoram

Rs/Kg

Dealers	*Particulars*	*Garlic*	*Onion*	*Potato*	*Turmeric Powder*
Wholesaler	Average Cost Price	82.82	40.95	17.9	191.5
	Average Selling Price	93.16	50.09	20.43	211
	Profit Margin	10.34	9.14	2.53	19.5
	Profit Margin (%)	12.48	22.32	14.13	10.18
Retailer	Average Cost Price	95.15	50.5	20.73	216.8
	Average Selling Price	120	59.15	26.35	259.3
	Profit Margin	24.85	8.65	5.62	42.5
	Profit Margin (%)	26.12	17.13	27.11	19.60
Wholesale + Retail Average	Average Cost Price	88.99	45.73	19.32	203.9
	Average Selling Price	106.58	54.62	23.39	235.15
	Profit Margin	17.59	8.89	4.07	31.25
	Profit Margin (%)	19.77	19.44	21.07	15.33

Source: Market Survey during November 2013 – January 2014.

Conclusion

Items considered in this chapter are the basic vegetable and fruit items of the people in the state and hence, the condition of its supply should be of crucial importance for the policy makers. Absence of efficient market mechanism could adversely affect the people, especially the poor. Some of the observations that could be made on the basis of the preceding analysis are as follows:

First, in spite of it being the staple food items of the people, there is no regulated market mechanism for these commodities to check price increase and to facilitate regular flow of supply. The producers as well as the consumers are exposed to the gut of open market frequented by a network of intermediaries, which results in high prices with uncertainty on quality delivery and un-remunerative price earned by the producers.

Second, there is no organised marketing institution from either the private or public sector to facilitate marketing of these commodities. The study found a good scope for the introduction of modern marketing chains of vegetables and fruits in the state. This would include contract farming, emergence of facilitative NGOs and Self Help Groups (SHGs), private investment, etc.

Third, the study revealed that the growers sell their produce right after harvest to the available market agents due to lack of appropriate cold storage facility in the cultivating areas. Alongside this, there is no available storage facility even for the dealers at the market stations. Quantity of products arrived in the market are quickly disposed-off because the sellers prefer to rush sale through heavy price reduction rather than incur losses from spoilage. It is safe to assume that substantial amount of the commodity that arrive in the market is spoiled every day resulting in losses for the stakeholders. The situation is also believed to be true for fruits as well as fish. The state has to rely on the import of the vegetables, which it produces in large quantity, from other states and Myanmar because of inadequate arrangement that could ensure uninterrupted flow of supply.

Fourth, there is no arrangement for the adoption of proper packaging and handling in accordance with the delicacy of the locally produced items. The significance of these arrangements could be seen from the conditions of imported vegetable items of potato, turmeric, onion, and garlic. Since these items are properly packaged (at least in semi-processed form) before it enters into the local market, various market agents have the opportunity to stock them for a longer period, and hence ensure stable prices and profit margins among the various market agents and even for the consumers. Besides providing facilities for proper packaging and handling, refrigerated transport (cold van) is essential for transportation of delicate items like fish to distant places without deterioration of its quality.

Fifth, the study did not find sufficient infrastructure for promoting fruit processing in the state. With more and more areas coming under fruit cultivation since the implementation of NLUP in 2011, establishing fruit canning and processing units by the public or private sector is necessary to cope with the anticipated increase in production in the next few years. It was also observed that there is a good market avenue for local fish and fruit products at other states, especially in Assam. To explore these opportunities, local producers should be equipped with better marketing infrastructure and be enhanced with required skill for post-harvest management of their produce.

5

General Conclusions

Increased agricultural production in the absence of efficient market mechanism could worsen the stake of farm population, rather than alleviate their hardship and poverty. Well established and organised marketing institutions and channels, which ensure better flow of commodity movement and distribution of value chain among various stakeholders starting from producers to retailers, are required to cope with the increasing production of agriculture and allied sector in the state. However, such marketing structure is not easy to achieve in the state considering the diverse nature of marketing channels with insufficient infrastructure being the main problem for most of the cases. In a nutshell, all such imperfect scenario of commodity marketing conditions in the state are indicated in this study.

The importance of agriculture market regulations to protect the interest of the farmers was recognised since long time back in the state, and necessary initiatives were undertaken by the Mizo District Council by passing 'The Mizoram District (Market) Regulation 1954' and 'The Mizo District (Market) Rules 1956'. Several legislations were passed in respect of agricultural marketing even after the Mizo District was upgraded to Union Territory Status in 1972 and its subsequent up-gradation to be a full-fledged State in 1987. However, a successful market regulation is hard to come by in Mizoram because marketing of agriculture and allied produce are still at the hands of unorganised network of middlemen and traders. The existing institutions in the public sector like Trade and Commerce Department, MAMCO Ltd, MIFCO Ltd, etc. have not been able to ensure smooth and efficient flow of agricultural produce to the end users which also results in unremunerated returns to the farmers. At the same time, several market intervention initiatives by the State government through these institutions usually fail to achieve its goals.

Moreover, the contribution of most of the cooperative societies, except MULCO for dairy milk, is quite minimal in promoting agriculture marketing. Consequently, the only agents at work are the few organised private establishments (HCP, ZEP, etc) and producer associations (MIGA, ZAGS), and the complex network of middlemen (local and non-local), commission agents, retailers, etc. At the same time, associations of local commission agents and the retailer associations in some market places are actively working in their respective jurisdiction and generally cartelise the commodity prices to protect the interest of their own members. Accordingly, there is no regulated market mechanism even for the common food items (vegetables) to check price increase and to facilitate regular flow of supply. The producers as well as consumers are exposed to the market controlled by a network of these intermediaries, which results in high prices of commodities with uncertainty on quality delivery and unremunerated prices earned by the producers. Taking into account the failure of the state in regulating the market in the past, re-evaluation of the various strategies adopted by the government is necessary to chalk out improved and applicable marketing regulations. At this time of economic liberalisation, the roles played by private investments in market reorganisation should also be taken into account.

Lack of adequate infrastructure in the form of means of communication, transportation, storage, etc. hampers the smooth flow of commodity markets in the state. Items that get spoiled easily seldom arrive in the market from the interior areas. Even the quantities that arrived are, most of the time, insufficient to cater the demand level in the market. Moreover, all surplus production areas of locally produced vegetable items, which are grown across the state, are in and around the main roads connecting important towns and the city where there are regular transport services. This follows that producers in the far flung areas do not have the opportunity to sell their surplus products due to inadequate storage and transport facility, which otherwise would have arrived in the market and improve the supply conditions. In addition, there is no effective mechanism in place for dissemination of market information among the various stakeholders and this would undermine the decision making process of the producers as well as other marketing agents.

There is no adequate storage facility available for dealers trading in the market stations. Quantity of products arrived in the market, therefore, has to be quickly disposed-off because the sellers prefer to rush sale through heavy price reduction rather than incur losses from spoilage. It was found that substantial amount of the commodity that arrive in the market is spoiled every day. Anticipating the need for rush sale, usually done at the end of the day, and to cover up the anticipated loss, the retailers charge relatively higher prices resulting in consumer's surplus loss on the part of the consumer. Further, local vegetables items that can be stored for relatively longer period like brinjal, bean, etc. were found to have better producers' share in the consumer price. This clearly suggests the improvement of efficiency in market flow with increase in the retaining capacity of the producer as well as other stakeholders. Thus, the emergence of adequate storage facilities at least in the major market destinations of the state, either from the public or the private sector, would improve the marketing conditions of agriculture produce in the state.

It is a common practice among the farmers in Mizoram to sell their produce in unprocessed form without performing even the simplest post-harvest activities of grading, sorting, packing, etc., although sufficient technological and infrastructural arrangements to promote such activities is absent. The realised prices by the producers were found to be relatively higher for such commodities in which the producers conduct at least the basic post-harvest management and value addition activities. For example, the producers' shares in the consumer prices are significantly higher in case of anthurium flowers and brooms where basic post-harvest technologies were imposed. The same is the case for lemon (nimbu) even if it is processed by simple local technology. Further, as imported items like potato, onion, and garlic are normally in their semi-processed form, relatively stable distribution chain of prices and profits through the different stakeholders were also observed in these cases. Thus, it is necessary that the practice of post-harvest management activities emerge among the producers through public policy measures and entry of private investments.

The value chain analysis of the selected 20 agriculture and allied products in Mizoram shows the advantage of well-organised marketing institutions and channels as indicated by higher producer's share in the final price, while it is lower in the case of unorganised market channels. Examples are the cases of the brooms and areca-nut (betel nut). The former is marketed through a well-organised marketing channel (i.e. HCP) while the latter is characterised by non-transparent and unorganised channels. The advantage of organised market channels are relatively higher producer's share in the final price, and generation of employment opportunities in the process of value addition by various stakeholders. At the same time, marketing of areca-nut shows unnecessary transit via Assam on account of intermediary intervention in its process resulting in low producer's share in the final price with the consumer being the loser.

A peculiar feature of agricultural commodity market is that the state's capital Aizawl remains to be the main market terminal for most of the items, whether imported or procured from within the state. It serves as the main feeder for all other big markets in the state. For example, garlic or onion imported from Myanmar through Champhai town would first come to the hands of wholesalers dealing in Aizawl city, and the same would be purchased by retailers from different parts of the state, even by the retailers from villages located near Champhai town. One reason for this could be the existence of regular maxi-cab services from most of the villages to Aizawl, and not to big towns or district headquarters nearer to them. If this is so, it is much easier to purchase such commodity from Aizawl rather than the nearby towns irrespective of the distance.

The cases of re-imported items (agricultural produce exported to other states, but are imported again in processed or semi-processed form) need appropriate attention. As noted earlier, areca-nut is exported to Assam and is again imported in semi-processed form from Assam state with higher wholesale price. The same is the case for orange imported during the off-season (monsoon). The unnecessary transit of these items via other states makes both the farmers and consumer losers. It is suggested that the volume of local demand throughout the year may be examined, and necessary steps be taken to create storage facilities at least to accommodate these quantities. In fact, several initiatives of the government in respect of marketing have failed due to management failure in most of the cases. Thus, utmost care should be taken in selection of the strategy for such initiatives, while the scope of Public Private Partnership (PPP) mode may also be investigated.

The study observed impressive geographical spread of production for local vegetable and fruit items, giving scope of self-sufficiency in these items throughout the year. To leverage this opportunity, modern system of cultivation and marketing (e.g. contract farming, buy-back system, etc.) has to be evolved in the state. Such initiatives may be extended to crops like potato, onion, garlic, fish, etc. in which the state is heavily dependent on outside source. This may be made possible by the state government by making facilitative legal provisions, while the financial requirements may come through attractive credit facilities from financial institutions.

In summary, the analysis made in this study revealed the unsustainable system of agriculture marketing with frequent intervention by unnecessary intermediaries and middlemen in the state resulting in low producer's share in the final price. In fact, a relatively more established channel like the ones at work for broom and anthurium certainly provide stable market avenues for the farmers; even though there still is a wide area for enhancement of earnings in the process of value addition for these items. Inadequate storage facility inhibited the smooth supply flow resulting in inflated prices paid by the consumers, while the retailers incur losses due to heavy price reduction resulting from unavailability of infrastructure to protect commodities from spoilage. The techniques of post-harvest management in terms of packaging, grading, and the like are essential for safe transportation of products.

Bibliography

Acharya, S.S. and Agarwal, N.L. (1987), *Agricultural Marketing in India,* First Edition, Oxford and IBH Publishing Co. Pvt. Ltd., New Delhi.

Arya, Anita (1993), *Agricultural Marketing in Gujarat,* Concept Publishing Company, New Delhi.

Auyasami U and Bohle, H.G. (1981),'Market Access as constraints on Marginal and Small Farmers', *Economic and Political Weekly* Vol. 16. No. 13.

Chakraborty, Kiran Sarkar (2009), *Rural Market and Agricultural Marketing—A case study of Tripura,* Mittal Publications, New Delhi.

Community Development Action and Reflection (2012), *CDAR Records 2012.*

Bezbaruah, M.P. (2009), 'Indo-Myanmar Border Trade: The stakes for North East India', *Dialogue, A Quarterly Journal of Astha Bharati.*

Dantwala, M.L. (1966), 'Principles and Problems of Agricultural Price Determination', *Indian Journal of Agricultural Economics, June.*

Dave, P.K. (1980), *Risk and Uncertainty in Indian Agriculture,* Unpublished PhD Thesis, Gujarat University.

Deigharia, P.C. (2011), 'Vegetable Marketing in Jharkhand', *Jharkhand Journal of Social Develoopment,* Vol. 4, No. 1 and 2.

Deole, C.D. (1979), 'An Analysis of Wheat Price difference in Regulated markets', *Indian Journal of Agricultural Economics,* Oct-Dec.

Fletcher, James (1990), 'Public interventions in Agricultural Markets in Malaysia: Rice and Palm Oil', *Modern Asian Studies,* Vol. 24, No. 2.

George, Leena (1996), *The Ginger Economy of Kerala,* Unpublished PhD Thesis of Department of Applied Economics, Cochin University of Science and Technology, Kochi.

Ghatak, S and Ingersent, K (1984), *Agriculture and Economic Development,* Select Book Service Syndicate, New Delhi.

Govt. of Mizoram (2011), *Mizoram Border Trade and Myanmar and Bangladesh,* Directorate of Trade and Commerce Department.

—— (2011), *A Bird's eye view of Trade and Commerce Department 2011,* Directorate of Trade and Commerce Department.

—— (2011), *General Reports of MAMCO Ltd 1993-2011,* Mizoram Agricultural Marketing Corporation Limited (MAMCO).

—— (2011), *Citizens' Charter 2012,* Directorate of Trade and Commerce Department.

—— Various Issues of *Economic Survey,* Department of Planning and Programme Implementation Department.

—— Various Issues of *Basic Statistics* and *Statistical Abstract of Mizoram*, Directorate of Economics and Statistics, Mizoram.

Hariss, Barbara (1979), *Paddy and Rice Marketing in Northern Tamil Nadu*, Sangam Publihser, Madras.

Jairat, M.S. (2000), 'Agricultural Marketing Infrastructures in India', *Agricultural Situations in India*, Vol. XVI, June. Directorate of Economics and Statistics, Department of Agriculture and Cooperation, Government of India.

Kakaty, G. (2009), 'Potentialities of Horticultural Crops and Market Accessibilities in Assam and Meghalaya with Special Reference to Technology Mission for Integrated Development of Horticulture', Agro-Economic Research Centre for North East India, Jorhat, Study No. 130.

Kakaty, Gautam and Debajit Borah (2011), *Impact of Emerging Marketing Channels in Agriculture Benefit to Producer-Sellers and the Marketing Costs and Margins of Orange and Potato in Assam*, Study No. 139 of Agro-Economic Research Centre for North East India, Assam Agriculture University.

Laldinpuii, K. (2013), 'The Frontier Market and their Roles', in Malsawmdawngkima and Rohmingmawii (Eds) *Mizo Narratives: accounts from Mizoram*, Scientific Book Centre, Guwahati.

Lalngaizuala (2001), 'Kan Sawhthing hi', *Vanglaini*, Vol. XVII, No. 129.

Lawmthanga (1997), *Thlaithar Hralhna (Agricultural Marketing)*, Mizoram Economy Series-I, MCL Publications, Aizawl.

Lianzela and Thangchungnunga (1996), 'Solution of Marketing Problems in Mizoram Part I and II', *Ram Kalsiam-15*, Synod Social Front Committee, Aizawl.

MIGA (2013), *Records of the activities of MIGA*, Mizoram Iskut Growers' Association, Sihphir, Mizoram.

Moore, J.R.; Kohl, S.S. and Khusro (1973), *Indian Foodgrains Marketing*, Prentice Hall of India Pvt. Ltd, New Delhi.

NABARD (2010), *State Focus Paper 2010-11*, Mizoram, Aizawl.

Pachouri, Anshul (2012), 'Economic Inefficiencies in Farm-Market Linkages in Agriculture Value Chain in India: Problems and Solutions', *ISAS Working Paper*, No. 163. Institute of South Asian Studies, Singapore.

Pandey, M.K. (1982), *Marketing Efficiency of Food Grain in Gujarat*, Unpublished PhD Thesis, Gujarat University.

Pandey, N.K., Arun Pandi, Nalini R. Kumar and R.K. Rana (2003), 'Price Spread Analysis of Potato Marketing at Shimla', *Journal of Indian Potato Association*, 30 (1-2).

Panwar, N.D. and Mishal, D.H. (2005), 'Behaviour of Prices and Arrivals of Pomegranate in Western Maharashtra, *Agricultural Marketing, A national level quarterly Journal on Agricultural Marketing*, Directorate of Marketing and Inspection, Ministry of Agriculture, Government of India, Vol. XLVII, No. 4.

Rajagopalan, V. (1968), 'Farm Liquidity and Institutional financing for

Agricultural Development', *Indian Journal of Agricultural Economics,* Vol. XXII, Oct.-Dec.

Rao, Hanumantha and Subbarao, K. (1976), 'Marketing of Rice in India', *Indian Journal of Agricultural Economics,* April-June 1976.

Reddy, K.R. (1995), *Marketing of Chillies (Eds),* Rupa Books Pvt. Limited, Tilak Nagar, Jaipur.

Rhodes, J.V. (1978), *The Agricultural marketing system in Columbia,* Grid Publishing.

Rohmingliani and Thanga, JLT (2014), 'Marketing Efficiency of Anthurium Cut Flowers in India: An Analysis', *Management Convergence,* Vol. 5, No. 1 and 2.

Rualzakhuma (2002), *The status of agricultural marketing in Mizoram and the urgent need for evolving a new and stable long term policy,* Seminar paper dated 4.9.2002 organized by IIPA Mizoram Regional Branch, Aizawl.

Saha, Niranjan (1986), 'Land system and agricultural development in the hills of North East India', B.B. Dutta and M.N. Karna (Eds) *Land Relation in North East India.*

Sarkar, D. and Mondal, R.C. (2011), *Impact of Emerging marketing channels in agricultural marketing: benefit to producer-seller and marketing costs and margins of agricultural commodities—A study in West Bengal,* Agro-Economic Research Centre, Visva-Bharati, Santiniketan.

Shukla, S.P. and Agarwal, A.K. (1986), *Agriculture in North Eastern Region,* First Edition, National Publishing House, 23 Darya Ganj, New Delhi.

Singh, S. and Chauhan, S.K. (2004), 'Marketing of vegetables in Himachal Pradesh', *National Level Quarterly Journal on Agriculture Marketing,* Vol. XLVII, No. 3, Directorate of Marketing and Inspection, Ministry of Agriculture, Government of India.

Singh, Sikander and Rangi, P.S. (2010), 'Marketing Problems of Sunflower in Punjab', *Political Economy Journal of India,* Vol. 19, January-June.

Singh, Balwinder (2000), *Agricultural Credit-Sources, Problems and Emerging Issues,* Deep and Deep Publications Pvt Ltd., New Delhi.

Talukdar, K.C. and Bhowmick, B.C. (1993), *Marketing of Perishable Products (Eds),* B.R. Publishing Corporation, New Delhi.

Thanga, J.L.T. (2014), *Agriculture Production and Market Survey,* Unpublished Research Project, Department of Economics, Mizoram University, Aizawl.

Vanrammawia, K. and Thanga, JLT (2013), 'Marketing of Ginger in Mizoram', *Management Convergence,* Vol. 4, No. 2.

Vanrammawia, K. and Thanga, JLT (2014), 'Marketing Pattern of Squash and the Role of Growers Association of Mizoram', *Geographic,* Vol. 9, July.

Zonuntluanga, R. (2002), *Problems and Prospects of Agricultural Marketing in Mizoram,* Unpublished PhD Thesis, Department of Economics, Mizoram University, Aizawl.

Zorema, J. (2012), Agricultural Marketing and Economic Development—A Study of Mizoram. Mittal Publications, New Delhi.

Index